Ministry of the Sacred Artist

Julious Fletcher

MINISTRY OF THE SACRED ARTIST

ISBN: 978-0-9889346-0-3

CONTENTS

ACKNOWLEDGMENTS

To my Heavenly Father, who gave me the ability for me to operate and articulate the ministry that He gave me and assist those in the liturgical arts.

To my parentals, Melvin and Servetus Fletcher, I thank you for your love and support from the both of you. In everything that I have done, you have fully supported me and have given me your prayers.

To my godmother, Annette Patterson (Queen Mother), I appreciate your assistance and sacrifice in all that you have done to support me in life and in ministry. It is not unnoticed.

To Apostle O. Saint Ekoh and Dr. Cynthia Ekoh, you are the best Pastor and First Lady that I could ever have. You have supported me and pushed me for the better. Along with you, the rest of my church family, Jesus Lighthouse, I appreciate each and every one of you for the love and support that you show to me.

To Pastor David Twyman for being my accountability partner as well as pushing me to complete this book.

To Michelle Lewis and Moneka Dixon for assisting me in editing this book.

To Rekesha Pittman for the guidance to make this book possible.

To Yakeisha Biggs for the book cover.

INTRODUCTION

There is a generation that is rising that does not understand the liturgical arts ministry. Some people will look at this ministry as a joke. I wanted to bring clarity to people who do not understand the liturgical arts ministry and teach them the truth. My goal is not to bewitch you and give you traditional and religious doctrine regarding the arts ministry. I want you to be able to live, move and have your being in this ministry. Some of you that are reading this book because liturgical ministry is new for you; some of you have purchased this book because it is a refresher course. This ministry is one of the abused ministries in the Body of Christ because it is seen as entertainment and not as pure ministry. Reader, I pray that after you read the chapters in this book, you will understand that this ministry is a serious ministry just as the pulpit ministry. This is not to be taken lightly, but I pray that fear does not come upon you and make you fearful at the same time. God is a creative God. We see God's creativity when He created the Earth, the sun and moon and all of nature, as well as the universe. We serve a creative God, so let us worship Him in creativity as well.

Chapter One
History of the Arts

In the beginning God created the heaven and the earth. And the earth was without form, and void; and darkness was upon the face of the deep. And the Spirit of God moved upon the face of the waters
(King James Version, Genesis 1:1-2).

In the beginning God used His creativity to form the heaven and the earth. When the earth was without form, the Holy Spirit moved over the face of the waters. *Moved* comes from the Hebrew word *rachaph*. *Rachaph* means "to brood; by implication to be relaxed: -flutter, move, shake." This signifies that the Holy Spirit danced on the face of the waters.

Therefore, from the beginning, the arts have been an expression of God's presence. God ordained the arts to express His will in the earth. Before man was created, God had someone else to handle the arts (or the worship) in Heaven.

"Son of man, take up a lament concerning the king of Tyre and say to him: This is what the Sovereign LORD says:

"'You were the seal of perfection,

full of wisdom and perfect in beauty.
You were in Eden,
   the garden of God;
every precious stone adorned you:
   carnelian, chrysolite and emerald,
   topaz, onyx and jasper,
   lapis lazuli, turquoise and beryl,
Your settings and mountings were made of gold;
   on the day you were created they were prepared.
¹⁴ *You were anointed as a guardian cherub,*
   for so I ordained you.
You were on the holy mount of God;
   you walked among the fiery stones.
¹⁵ *You were blameless in your ways*
   from the day you were created
   till wickedness was found in you.
¹⁶ *Through your widespread trade*
   you were filled with violence,
   and you sinned.
So I drove you in disgrace from the mount of God,
   and I expelled you, guardian cherub,
   from among the fiery stones.
¹⁷ *Your heart became proud*
   on account of your beauty,
and you corrupted your wisdom
   because of your splendor.

So I threw you to the earth;

I made a spectacle of you before kings

(New International Version, Ezekiel 28:13-17).

We see in this scripture that Lucifer was in the Garden of Eden. According to verse 14, he was <u>anointed</u> as a guardian cherub. This indicates that in order for anyone to operate in the worship arts, you have to be anointed for this. Cherubs are angels that are associated with the presence of God; they are also protective with the things of God. We see this in Scriptures:

After he drove the man out, he placed on the east side of the Garden of Eden cherubim and a flaming sword flashing back and forth to guard the way to the tree of life (New International Version, Gen 3:24).

And make two cherubim out of hammered gold at the ends of the cover. [19] Make one cherub on one end and the second cherub on the other; make the cherubim of one piece with the cover, at the two ends. [20] The cherubim are to have their wings spread upward, overshadowing the cover with them. The cherubim are to face each other, looking toward the cover. [21] Place the cover on top of the ark and put in the ark the tablets of the covenant law that I will give you. [22] There, above the cover between the two cherubim that are over the ark of the covenant law, I will meet with you and give you all my commands for the Israelites (New International Version, Ex 25:18-22).

LORD Almighty, the God of Israel, enthroned between the cherubim, you alone are God over all the kingdoms of the earth. You have made heaven and earth (New International Version, Is 37:16).

Lucifer's role was to lead worship in Heaven. As we can see, Lucifer (Satan) was blameless until his heart became proud because of his beauty, and he corrupted his wisdom because of his splendor.

Isaiah 14: 12-15 says:

How you have fallen from heaven,
morning star, son of the dawn!
You have been cast down to the earth,
you who once laid low the nations!
You said in your heart,
"I will ascend to the heavens;
I will raise my throne
above the stars of God;
I will sit enthroned on the mount of assembly,
on the utmost heights of Mount Zaphon.
I will ascend above the tops of the clouds;
I will make myself like the Most High."
But you are brought down to the realm of the dead,
to the depths of the pit
(New International Version, Isaiah 14:12-15).

Lucifer stopped reflecting God and started reflecting himself, which is a show of pride. This is why it is important for <u>all</u> sacred artists to understand: any time you reflect yourself, you resemble Lucifer. His ending was that he was kicked out and replaced; do you want to share the same fate? When Lucifer was kicked out, he took 1/3 of heaven with him.

The great dragon was hurled down—that ancient serpent called the devil, or Satan, who leads the whole world astray. He was hurled to the earth, and his angels with him (New International Version, Rev 12:9).

When Satan was rejected, God brought a replacement: us.

Then God said, "Let us make mankind in our image, in our likeness, so that they may rule over the fish in the sea and the birds in the sky, over the livestock and all the wild animals, and over all the creatures that move along the ground." So God created mankind in his own image, in the image of God he created them; male and female he created them. (New International Version, Genesis 1:26-27)

It is important that we worship God because we were made in the image of God. When God looks at us, He sees Himself. Anytime you look in a mirror, you see yourself or if you are a parent and you look at your children, you see yourself. That is the same thing with God, which is why God desires an intimate relationship with us.

When it comes to the arts (or the ministry of the arts), Ezekiel 28:13 links the jewels of the high priest that we now wear, which show that we here been given the same authority to operate.

You were in Eden,
  the garden of God;
every precious stone adorned you:
  carnelian, chrysolite and emerald,
  topaz, onyx and jasper,
  lapis lazuli, turquoise and beryl.

Your settings and mountings were made of gold;
  on the day you were created they were prepared.

God is a God of specific and these nine stones are specific. Lucifer (Satan) was dressed in this at the beginning. When he was kicked out of Heaven, God gave us Lucifer's job description. Now, to actually signify that we have that job description, God gave us those nine stones as well yet he added three more. We know these stones are on the High Priest's breastplate, which are also the stones of the Twelve Tribes of Israel. The number 12 is God's divine government and authority so when God gave us these stones, He gave us governmental authority to lead worship.

Then mount four rows of precious stones on it. The first row shall be carnelian, chrysolite and beryl; the second row shall be turquoise, lapis lazuli and emerald; the third row shall be jacinth, agate and amethyst; the fourth row shall be topaz, onyx and jasper (Exodus 28: 17-20a)

God's message in this is that we have the authority to set things in order when it comes into the ministry of the arts as well as to continue to add and be fruitful while representing Jesus.

For in him all things were created: things in heaven and on earth, visible and
invisible, whether thrones or powers or rulers or authorities; all things have been
created through him and for him (New International Version, Col 1: 16b).

Everything created was for God and His purpose. Look at the physical history of other characteristics of the arts.

Now, I want to discuss <u>step</u> (or <u>drill</u>). Step was created back by African-Americans in slavery; like hymns, slaves used step to communicate to each other by using African dance. Step incorporates spoken word, music and dance. It became a culture of its own; after the slaves were freed, it evolved to fraternities and sororities using this as a form of entertainment, along with the growing music industry of Motown and the early stages of R&B and hip-hop music. (Wallace 1998). Now, we in the Kingdom, want to use this same art form to give God glory. The important thing is you need to know how to use it and when to use it or you will abuse it.

Next, I want to discuss <u>mime</u>. Mime is a physical display of storytelling without words; the ancient Greeks and Romans did this in the theatre in the form of masks. As it evolved through time in the Middle Ages, it was used to make fun of people in society and would not be able to get into trouble because no one knew who the person was (Nielsen 1993).

For this art form, there are two types of mime: literal and abstract mime. Literal mime has a plot or a storyline; abstract involves acting out emotions and thoughts on a particular subject without a plot

(Nielsen 1993).

In Biblical aspects, we see that the old prophets would act out certain things so the people of God would understand what God was saying. Ezekiel 3:26 actually says God cleaved Ezekiel's tongue to the roof of his mouth so many messages he was trying to covey had to be acted out. Hosea also refers to parables as well as being married to a harlot for the message of Israel's infidelity to be known. In the New Testament, we also see a mime demonstration in Acts 21:11.

In today's time, when it comes into the white make up, it is used to cover the face especially on stage so the facial expressions could be accented. In ministry, we say that the face is being covered because the person is shedding him or herself so God may be displayed.

Poetry or spoken word is a form of literature that was used for passing history and stories. It was another form of communication. There are three forms of poetry: lyric, dramatic, and narrative (Uttley 1998).

Lyrical poetry displays the mood or emotions of the writer. It was accompanied with music (mostly a lyre). We can pull this from Shakespeare's sonnets; Ancient Greeks used this form for the chorus to sing during plays (Uttley 1998).

Dramatic works would be written in verse which would be what some playwrights used such as William Shakespeare's *A Midsummer Night's Dream* (Uttley 1998).

Narrative works would be long poems that talks about a specific situation and some poems in this category are known as epics. We know epic poems such as Homer's *Iliad* and the *Odyseey* (Greek) and Chaucer's *The Canterbury Tales* (English) (Uttley 1998). As time continued, poetry evolved to where the world recognized some great poets and English classes today still study these as a part of the curriculum.

 In the Biblical aspect, poetry is displayed in the Book of Psalms as well as Song of Solomon; Psalms is known as songs and prayers as well as poetic forms. Song of Solomon, however, is a love poem between two lovers communicating their love for each other using imagery.

This chapter was very important because you must understand the history behind the ministry you are actively participating in; I wanted you to have a clear understanding of where everything comes so you will be able to inform people of your artistic history.

Chapter Two

Knowing Your Assignment

And the Lord answered me and said, Write the vision and engrave it so plainly upon tablets that everyone who passes may [be able to] read [it easily and quickly] as he hastens by. For the vision is yet for an appointed time and it hastens to the end [fulfillment]; it will not deceive or disappoint. Though it tarry, wait [earnestly] for it, because it will surely come; it will not be behindhand on its appointed day (Habakkuk 2:2-3).

In this section, I want to discuss your vision and purpose as an arts ministry. In order for you to start this process, you must first hear God. He will validate the purpose and vision that He gives you. As an arts ministry, we should follow the five "W"s and one "H": Who are you (What is your name), What do you do, Why do you do that you do, When are you going to do it, Where are you going to do and How are you going to implement it.

Who are you? What is your name of the ministry? God would always give you a name for your ministry and He would connect that to His word. It is important that all arts ministries are based on the Word of God. This is your foundation; if your foundation is not based on the

Word of God, then it will fall. Understand that it is important that your name actually has a meaning behind it. Who you are is connected to your purpose in the ministry.

What do you do? What is the purpose God has called you into this particular ministry? Whenever God wants to fulfill a need, He would call someone to fulfill it. What is the need that you need to fulfill? In the arts ministry, we should have a vision and a purpose for existing. We should not have the generic vision statement as other arts ministries such as "seeing souls saved, people delivered and healed." The truth with this generic vision is that all forms of ministries and all believers should cater to the commandment that Jesus said (see Matthew 28:19-20).

The problem with some arts ministries is that they form and they copy someone else's vision. It doesn't work this way. Your particular arts ministry should have a specific purpose on why you exist. If you copy someone else's vision, then you begin to operate in an area that God never intended for you to operate in. This means if you do anything outside of your area, God is not obligated to assist you because He didn't tell you do that. The ability for you to operate in someone else's vision as if it was your own will not be there.

Please understand that different arts ministries have different functions. The purpose and vision for one arts ministry will not be the same as another. For example, one art ministry's purpose is specifically to go out and do outreach in the community. Another's purpose may just be to do shows and teaching basic biblical principles thru the arts. A different one may just do warfare pieces to pull down strongholds within the community. If one doesn't know the function of the ministry, abuse will happen.

Why do you do it? The generic fashion is that we come together to glorify God with our bodies. Everyone in the Body of Christ should be doing that but what is the specific reason that you are doing this particular type of ministry. Is it because you want to be seen? Is it because you need special attention? Is it because you are doing it because God called you to this ministry to make a difference? Is it because you committed yourself to this ministry because you love God? Is it because of traumatic past experiences and God is using the arts to minister to you and the people so you (and the people) can be healed from it? There are a lot of reasons why we are involved in this ministry. Be aware of your objectives and your motives in this type of ministry because you are always in front of an audience.

Where are you going to do it? This deals with location. Where are you going to minister to this specific need? Is the reason that the ministry exists is because it is needed within the four walls of the church? Is the reason for you to go out into the community and touch lives with the arts? Is it for you to gain fame and fortune? Is it for you to go all over the world and preach the Gospel thru the arts? You have to know where you are going.

If this is an arts ministry that it is only supposed to be within the four walls of the church, then the arts ministries' purpose and vision should follow under the vision of the pastor and have the shepherd's heart. It is also imperative that your leadership (pastor) knows why the arts ministries exist in that local assembly.

Sadly, some pastors don't understand the full intent of arts ministries and they just want to say "We have a dance ministry here and we represent!" Some pastors think that it is a filler for services; some think it is an extracurricular activity or something for the youth to do. Others think that it is just a form of entertainment. Whatever the Head leads, the rest of the body follows.

When are you going to do it? You also need to know the timing for you to launch out and operate in the ministry. Even though Samuel anointed David, David's time had not yet come for him to be a warrior/giant slayer and then reign as king. He went back to what he was doing: shepherding. This is a part of keeping your heart pure.

How are you going to accomplish it? Every ministry should have a strategic plan for strategic takeover. If you are like me, I love to have my ducks in a row before I present anything to my leadership. Along with any and every vision, you must have a plan on how you are going to accomplish the vision as well as how you are going to operate in this. This would also include if you are requiring the arts ministry to go to an arts conference to edify the ministry for them to learn how to use their gifts connecting with the vision of the ministry. Now that we have established about the ministry, let's deal with your audience.

Who are you ministering to? You have to know who your audience is. God raised you up to fulfill a need to a particular group of people. This is the time where the world is not coming to the Church; therefore, we must go to the world. God would send some art ministries on national TV shows or secular professional art organizations such as theatres and concerts because God is trying to get His Word to people. Please listen to what I am saying. God would call someone out to make a difference in that arena. People complain about how demonic television shows have gotten and there are no good movies. Well, in order for a revolution to take place, He has to send someone that has His heart. The most important part is that we as an individual must know where God has called us to make an impact. Someone has to do it! It might as well be you.

If God has placed it in your heart to minister to people on professional platforms, by all means, go but don't be corrupted and stand firm on your foundation. Remember the reason why God chose you to go: to fulfill a need.

What are you ministering to this audience? What is the specific message God wants you to minister to the people? The message that you want to convey can be so many different things. If God has called you to go into the entertainment industry to cause a change within, then you need to know as the artist what message you want to convey to your audience.

Why are you ministering to this audience? Please know that the reason that you are ministering to this audience is for fulfilling a need. If God placed this need in your heart or if it is due to a past experience, it would be in this category. Also make sure that your passion is in this area as well. As I stated before, when it comes into people complaining about there is nothing good on television and no good movies. This is the area where if you are called in this arena and God has equipped you for that, then you should step in and do what you do.

When and where are you going to do? You have to know where you are going and when you are going to proactively engage in order to reach this audience. If you are doing this in ministry sake, then you need to know where in the community God is sending you to go fulfill the need. Not only where in the community, but also you need to know when you are going to do it. People are not moved by your lip service and you never do anything but they are more prone to support people who are actively doing something.

How are you going to do it? Again, your strategic plan should map out exactly what you want to have done. This is the time where you would need to sit and be still and hear God on how you can accomplish the vision as well as meet the need. Also, be watchful for the opportunity to appear and be ready for it to manifest before you.

Once you hear Him and He has fully spoken into your heart, then you would need to speak to your leadership if you haven't already. Sometimes, your leadership may already have the desire to have an arts ministry and they are waiting for someone to do it. After you have spoken to your leadership, then your leadership can cover you and support you in your endeavors of engaging what God has spoken into your heart.

Knowing your assignment is very important because if you don't know it, then you would fall for anything and do whatever that would come up instead of making an effective change.

Chapter Three

Cost of the Anointing

In this chapter, you must understand the four "P"s of the anointing: the purpose, the process, the price and the protection of the anointing.

Let us first establish what the anointing is.

Anointing is defined as:

> "to rub or sprinkle on; apply an unguent, ointment, or liquid to.to smear with any liquid; to consecrate or make sacred in a ceremony that includes the token applying of oil; to dedicate to the service of God" (Dictionary.com).

The purpose of the anointing is for a sacred task or assignment for that person's life; it isn't there for them to get noticed by millions and millions of people. It is placed in our lives to draw people to God. So when you are anointed for any task, that means you have been set apart for that particular reason. When you are anointed for dance ministry, that means that God has set you apart for His purpose in dance (or in the arts). In any country that has a governmental leader, whether a president, king, queen or emperor, there must be a ceremony to take place to solidify that person in that position. We, as ministers of the arts, must first be solidified by God in order for us to operate in the arts. We are operating under the King which is God and He must first solidify us so that we are to operate in this ministry. When He anointed you, He was saying that you are qualified and He has already placed in you what you need.

 Now you understand what the anointing is. We have to now discuss the purpose of the anointing. Sadly, people believe that the purpose the anointing is to make people holler, fall out and be spooky. This is not the purpose why God gave you the anointing.

The anointing is given to us for us to operate in servant hood. So when you operate in the anointing that God has given you, you are using it to minister to someone else. The anointing is not given to us for you to make a name for yourself, but it was given so you will have the grace (special endowment or special ability) to operate in the purpose God has set for you.

The Spirit of the Sovereign Lord is on me, because the Lord has anointed me to proclaim good news to the poor. He has sent me to bind up the brokenhearted, to proclaim freedom for the captives and release from darkness for the prisoners, to proclaim the year of the Lord's favor and the day of vengeance of our God, to comfort all who mourn, and provide for those who grieve in Zion—to bestow on them a crown of beauty instead of ashes, the oil of joy instead of mourning, and a garment of praise instead of a spirit of despair. They will be called oaks of righteousness, a planting of the Lord for the display of his splendor (New International Version, Isaiah 61:1-3).

When you are operating in the purpose of the anointing, then you will be called an "oak of righteousness" for His display. Oaks are trees that have endured the times and seasons and continued to be rooted and unmovable from where they have placed. Being an oak of righteousness means that you are confident in the anointing that God has placed in you and you have endured the race.

This is the purpose of the anointing on your life. Now, how do you obtain the anointing?

Let's look at the process of how the anointing oil was created.

Then the Lord said to Moses, "Take the following fine spices: 500 shekels[1] of liquid myrrh, half as much (that is, 250 shekels) of fragrant cinnamon, 250 shekels[1] of fragrant calamus, 500 shekels of cassia —all according to the sanctuary shekel—and a hin[1] of olive oil. Make these into a sacred anointing oil, a fragrant blend, the work of a perfumer. It will be the sacred anointing oil (New International Version, Exodus 30:22-25).

God is a God of purpose; there is a reason why He has five separate items to become one for the purpose of appointing someone to a task. The number five represents "grace." Grace is, as stated before, "special endowment and special ability." So when He has anointed us, He has given us the grace or the special ability to accomplish our task. This is why I can say that the anointing cannot be duplicated.

Let's look at these ingredients:

- Myrrah

  This ingredient was used as an embalmer so dead people would not stink. It was used to reduce swelling and stop pain. In order for myrrah to be extracted from a shrub, the branch must be broken. Once it is broken and myrrah is collected, it must be liquefied. It has to be placed through the fire (Zavada 2012).

  This shows us that in order for us to be anointed, this is a death walk to ourselves and we have to be broken in humility as well as going thru the Refiner's Fire.

- Cinnamon

  Cinnamon is harvested from the tree during the raining season. When it is wet, it is flexible and easier to work with it. It grows in wet, marsh lands next to flowing streams (Asaff 2006).

  With this ingredient, we have to go thru storms in our lives so that we would be easier to work with as well as able to flow with the Spirit of God.

- Calamus

Calamus is a herb that is commonly used for medicinal purposes and breaking addictions such as smoking. In ancient Egypt and India, it is known as an aphrodisiac. This item is harvested from marshy and swampy lands and is uprooted, split in half and dried up. (*Epicentre*).

We can say that we have valley seasons that we feel that God is far from us and we are not as passionate as we were before. It is necessary for these valley seasons because we have to understand that though we walk thru the valley of the shadow of death, we will fear no evil because He is still with us. We have the confidence that He is always with us even until the end of the age. This is also the drawing ingredient that will cause people to be drawn to you.

- Cassia

Cassia is related to the cinnamon; in order to harvest cassia, it requires the whole branch or the whole tree. (Asaff 2006).

This requires your complete participation; in order to be anointed, half of you won't do. This includes prayer, fasting, studying God's Word, private worship time as well as obedience and living a pleasing lifestyle to God.

- Olive Oil

Olive oil is taken from an evergreen tree and the leaves are crushed in order to produce the olive oil. (Olive Oil 2012).

There has to be a crushing to take place in your life. When we go through painful experiences, it's not meant to break you, but it is meant to get your "oil" out of you.

All of these items came from within something. This means that your anointing does not come from someone laying hands on you, but it comes from within you by going through trials and tribulations. This process was long, but it was worth it because God wanted excellence out of what was sacred unto Him.

Now that you see the purpose and process of the anointing, you need to know the price of it.

Mary took a pound of ointment of pure liquid nard [a rare perfume] that was very expensive, and she poured it on Jesus' feet and wiped them with her hair. And the whole house was filled with the fragrance of the perfume" (John 12:3).

The cost of this oil in ancient times was expensive. The anointing is not cheap! This is why we cannot allow cheap imitations to continue to flourish and have no true power behind it. A lot of time people want to be the leader, the dance leader, worldwide dancer, actor, writer, singer, poet, and director, but nine times out of ten, they don't want to pay for it with their life. We like to hold on to certain aspects of our lives because we have not properly healed from an issue that wounded us many years ago.

After discussing the purpose, process and price of the anointing, now you have to be protective of it.

"Some of them were in charge of the articles used in the temple service; they counted them when they were brought in and when they were taken out. Others were assigned to take care of the furnishings and all the other articles of the sanctuary, as well as the special flour and wine, and the oil, incense and spices. But some of the priests took care of mixing the spices" (New International Version, I Chronicles 9:28-30).

God shows us that He had protection of His articles in the temple. We ourselves are responsible for protecting our anointing. No one else is responsible for our passion or our anointing. Yes, we do need accountability, but we need to protect and guard ourselves.

God would say this to us about our anointing: protect and guard our hearts.

"As dead flies give perfume a bad smell, so a little folly outweighs wisdom and honor" (New International Version, Eccl. 10:1)

Why would God have Solomon state this if there were not a danger to protect your anointing?

So the gatekeepers' duty over the articles was to protect the oil unless the foreign objects got into the oil. Of course from the scripture it is stated, flies would come to the oil and they would die and they would stink up the whole tabernacle. Another thing about the situation is that once the fly has entered into the oil, it has made it unclean and then that oil has been contaminated and cannot be used; the process of making the anointing oil has to be started all over again.

We should make a commitment to be a vessel of honor (see II Timothy 2:21) and put aside any sin and weight that so <u>easily</u> beset us.

For example, in the summer, you already know that flies are crazy. It's like they wait at the door for you to open for them to come in. It is easy for the fly to come in, but you have to protect your food especially if you are outside barbequing.

Let's look at why the fly is pointed out:

According to *American Educator Encyclopedia*, man began to realize that the common fly "is one of the most dangerous and troublesome insects to afflict mankind. Houseflies are a nuisance and a health hazard. In the larval stage they carry tens of millions of bacteria and a newly formed adult fly carries about 1,000 bacteria, 500 on its body surface and 500 inside its body."

"It dissolves food by regurgitation on the food and then sucking the liquid through its proboscis, an appendage on its head. At the same time it is excreting the flyspecks (their droppings) containing the refuse of digestion plus the eggs and wormlike parasites of the intestines carried over the decaying matter the larvae used for food. It is said that in its lifetime a single fly can carry over six million germs."

"The average flight of the housefly is about six hundred yards but some may fly or be carried by the wind for several miles. This ability to fly from house to house and area to area, seeking food and warmth, makes them excellent carriers of disease."

This creature is a pest to us. It irritates us and lands on us whenever it sees fit, but overall, the flies in our lives are distractions.

What things in our lives are drawn to us and lingers until it actually gets into the oil? There are people and situations that are drawn to you because you are light in a dark place and the objective is to discrete the anointing on your life. Always understand they will get killed in the process, but if they land in the oil, you will have to go thru the anointing process again. God will always bring your enemies to your footstool and He has created you to be the Head and not the Tail.

What you need to know and recognize that certain things are distractions and will hinder us to process what you were created to be. You must protect what God has entrusted you with and use it for the right purposes. *It always protects (New International Version,* I Corinthians 13:7a); you say you love God and you love what you do, then you are willing to protect what God has given you.

Out of your rejection, abandonment, wounds, hurts and pain, God is causing the anointing process to happen in your life. Now that you know the cost of the anointing, are you willing to pay for it?

Chapter Four

Heart of the Sacred Artist

This is a ministry of always being in front of people; we have to go into the core reason of why you are doing the things that you are doing.

This is all connecting with motives. Dictionary.com states that *motives* are "something that causes a person to act in a certain way, do a certain thing, etc; the goal or object of a person's actions."

You must be wondering, in this chapter, why I am talking about motives. It is because entertainment and competition has come in the Body of Christ and we have left behind ministry.

Let's see the difference: According to *Webster*, *entertainment* is "to hold the attention of; amuse; divert." *Divert* means "to turn aside; deflect, as in direction, interest, or purpose." Entertainment connects with the word *performance*, which means "a presentation before spectators; any entertainment." Performance comes the word *perform* which means "to act in accord with the requirements or obligations of; fulfill; discharge, as a duty or promise."

Ministry however means "the office or duties of a minister" and a *minister* is "one who is authorized to preach, administer the sacraments, etc. in a church." That was the noun but the verb (a word that means action) means, "to provide for the wants and needs of someone."

So what does this all means? Worship arts ministries (dance, drama, music, mime, poetry, etc) exists to provide salvation, healing, deliverance and encouragement through expressions of worship and guide people to the throne and the presence of God; but when we operate in entertainment, we cause people to be deflected to another path. We become a stumbling block for those that need to be ministered instead of entertained.

Professional dancers and actors have no choice but to perform for people because it is their job and they have a contract to do that. They can do anything they want to in any attitude as long as the job gets done; when it comes to ministry, we are going before God in an act of worship (adoration) and to minister before God's people and our hearts have to be tested on why are we going before God's people with an impure heart.

Our focus has to change! If people want to be entertained, then tell them to watch television, go to movies or go to the theater. It is a time for everything Ecclesiastes 3 says but now is not the time for you to be entertained. We cannot supply the people of God and God entertainment when they need ministry.

It's very hardening to me where we have become performers to God and to the Body of Christ. I hate that because worship is intimacy with God and in the midst of where we are supposed to be intimate with God, we give Him amusement. We have forgotten our first love (see Rev. 2:4) and started to have impure motives for having a lot of these dance services and events and don't have a direct purpose for them.

This can play with a man's heart! We have started to allow the *So You Think You Can Dance* and *America 's Best Dance Crew* mentality to come in the midst of our worship. I speak of these shows not to degrade them but because there is a lot of showmanship and skill determination. Yes, we do need a balance between skill and Spirit but we cannot get so focused on skill and have little focus on Spirit and Spirit is our power. No matter what you do, skill will not have power until it is coupled with Spirit. We are in the world but we should not adapt to the world's way of thinking.

But God chose the foolish things of the world to shame the wise; God chose the weak things of the world to shame the strong (New International Version, I Cor. 1:27).

So now what is happening is that because we are not doing our job as a collective whole, God is using the foolish things to confound the wise. It was already foolish that people were getting saved, delivered, healed and encouraged by dance ministry pieces, dramas, and poetry. Now what He is doing is that He is using the most unlikely sources to glorify Him.

Due to entertainment and competition, this is causing division and disunity in the Body where we need the God of peace and unity to stand in and abound.

How good and pleasant it is when brothers live together in unity! It is like precious oil poured on the head, running down on the beard, running down on Aaron's beard, down upon the collar of his robes (New International Version, Psalm 133:1-2)

You see from this scripture that when we come into unity (verse one), then the anointing (the oil) can flow. Another instance of unity is Pentecost.

*And when the day of Pentecost was fully come, they were all with **one accord** in one place. And suddenly there came a sound from heaven as of a rushing mighty wind, and it filled all the house where they were sitting. And there appeared unto them cloven tongues like as of fire, and it sat upon each of them. And they were all filled with the Holy Ghost, and began to speak with other tongues, as the Spirit gave them utterance* (King James Version, Acts 2:1-4, emphasis added)

We cannot live, move and have our being as a unit unless we actually come together with one mindset, one vision, one goal, and one purpose. We cannot progress and build up the Kingdom of God if everybody has their own objectives and wants to build up their own kingdoms.

Yet a time is coming and has now come when the true worshipers will worship the Father in spirit and truth, for they are the kind of worshipers the Father seeks. God is spirit, and his worshipers must worship in spirit and in truth (New International Version, John 4:23-24)

Because the mindsets have gotten to *So You Think You Can Dance?*, *America's Best Dance Crew* and even *American Idol*, we have left the whole reason why we are doing this: to worship the Lord in Spirit and in Truth. Scripture stated that the Father is seeking for true worshippers; that means that false worshippers (performers) are in the midst of true worshippers. I strongly believe that this scripture is referring to "right now" more than ever. We have begun to treat worship as some type of fad and that this is the popular thing to do in churches and we haven't grasp the full purpose of why God ordained the arts to be placed in the church and why He set us apart to be ministers of the arts.

A man ought to examine himself before he eats of the bread and drinks of the cup (*New International Version,* I Corinthians 11:28)

Examine yourselves to see whether you are in the faith; test yourselves (*New International Version,* II Corinthians 13:5a)

for of the abundance of the heart his mouth speaketh (*King James Version,* Luke 6:45b)

Why are you doing the things that you are doing? What is your purpose for doing it? Are you doing the ministry because you just want to be paid or is it because it is your sincere worship to the Lord? How do we find out what you are operating in pure motives? It's by The Word of God because it's the Word of God that is the discerner of thoughts and intent of the heart

For the word of God is living and active. Sharper than any double-edged sword, it penetrates even to dividing soul and spirit, joints and marrow; it judges the thoughts and attitudes of the heart (*New International Version*, Hebrews 4:12)

If we use the Word of God to test what your heart is saying, then you can't go wrong.

We need to go back to the basics and rekindle the passion for Christ to worship Him through the arts because the love and the fellowship with the brethren have left the building. When we reconnect with the passion for Christ, then our need to fellowship with one another will follow.

Continue to seek God with a passion and that we worship God in Spirit and in Truth and we go back to the origin of why God called us to this ministry so that we may glorify Him as a unit.

Chapter Five

Choreography:

Manifesting Your Testimony

This [ark] contained a golden jar which held the manna and the rod of Aaron that sprouted and the [two stone] slabs of the covenant [bearing the Ten Commandments]. (Hebrews 9:4)

I love this revelation of the Ark of the Covenant and how it applies to the ministry of the arts.

First let's do some history on the Ark of the Covenant for those who don't know what the Ark of the Covenant was. Back in Exodus, after God delivered the children of Israel out of Egypt thru Moses, God told Moses to come up to the mountain so He would be able to give Moses the Ten Commandments so Moses would be able to teach the children of Israel. In that same time period, God also gave Moses instructions on how to construct His tabernacle and as well as the furniture within it. One of those pieces was the Ark of the Covenant. The purpose of the Ark of the Covenant was for God to meet with Moses or the high priest and God would speak to him about everything concerning the children of Israel (see Exodus 25.22). If you look at Israel's history, God's hand was manifested with the presence of the Ark of the Covenant. The Ark of the Covenant was the center of the Tabernacle. It was the essential part of the tabernacle because the Ark of the Covenant represents the presence and the power of God. This is what we need in order for peoples' lives to be changed.

Since we are New Testament believers and we no longer follow the Old Testament of sacrificing goats, pigeons, and lambs because of the blood of Jesus, we have to look at the New Testament of the Ark of the Covenant. There are three items that are stated in this scripture that we need to look at and apply this to our ministry. These three items are very significant for us to manifest the presence of God for our ministries and this have been broken down into stages on how we can invoke the presence of God. First, we need to discuss the two stone slabs of the covenant which were the Ten Commandments. This was concerning as "The law." This was the written word of God given to the people of God on how to live. Today, we have the Word of God (Old and New Testament). This would be concerned as the covenant for us. This is considered the *logos* state. *Logos* is Greek for "a *word*, being the expression of a *thought*, a saying." This is where we are studying the written Word of God. It is important that we have at least one scripture that can relate to the ministry piece that we are doing.

Then said the Lord to me, You have seen well, for I am alert and active, watching over My word to perform it. (Jeremiah 1:12)

God is moved by His Word. We cannot ask God to move in a piece and His Word is nowhere related to it. We must the study of God.

Study and be eager and do your utmost to present yourself to God approved (tested by trial), a workman who has no cause to be ashamed, correctly analyzing and accurately dividing [rightly handling and skillfully teaching] the Word of Truth (II Timothy 2:15)

Once you know that you have the Word hidden in your heart and it has been rooted, then you would be able to step into the next stage.

We have to know acknowledge *a golden jar which held the manna.* According to *The Student Bible Dictionary*, manna was "a whitish substance of nourishment that God provided for the Israelites during their forty years in the wilderness (Ex. 16.15). It remained after the morning dew evaporated and usually spoiled after one day. God instructed the Israelites to gather enough for one day with extra on the sixth day to provide for the Sabbath" (p 150). Now, this is what the children of Israel had to eat after they were liberated from Egypt. This is the next stage: after you have received and studied the written Word of God or *logos*, we step into the *rhema* stage. *Rhema* is Greek for "a *spoken* word, made "by the *living voice*"." This is the stage where we are seeing what God is saying to us and what is He saying thru our pieces. When we are in the *rhema* stage, this is where prayer is applied. Prayer is essential when it comes to the ministry of the arts because you must know what direction God is going. Prayer is just simply communication with God. So in order to please the One that we are working for, we must at least communicate with Him on a daily basis. This is important because the manna spoiled day after day so God would have to provide for the children of Israel continuously as they were in the wilderness. Your best choreography will not always come from dance school or a dance conference but it will come from your prayer time. For today's society, we must seek the face of God for a word daily because "we don't live by bread alone but every word that proceeds out of the mouth of God" (Matthew 4:4).

We have to acknowledge the vessel that the manna is in. It is a golden jar that is holding the Word of God. Gold represents "God's glory" and the jar (which is the vessel) represents us as the carriers of the revelatory Word of God (or the *rhema*, right now, Word of God).

However, we possess this precious treasure [the divine Light of the Gospel] in [frail, human] vessels of earth, that the grandeur and exceeding greatness of the power may be shown to be from God and not from ourselves (II Corinthians 4:7).

We have this treasure in earthly vessels. The reason that the vessel is overlaid with gold is because we want God's glory to overshadow us so the people will see Him and not us. When we don't know the Word that God is trying to say, then we are just entertaining the people and we are not conveying a message.

The last piece of the Ark of the Covenant we need to discuss is the *rod of Aaron that spouted*. Now the history lesson with the rod itself is that God would use the rod to do many miracles and wonders. So this rod itself represents "the power, authority or manifestation of

God." This stage would be the *dumas* or *excusia* stage. *Dumas* is Greek for " properly, "*ability* to perform"" and excusia is Greek for " authority, *conferred* power; *delegated empowerment* ("authorization"), operating in a *designated jurisdiction*." This is the power and authority stage. Now you need to know the significance of Aaron's rod. Due to the Korah rebellion and the people's complaints in Numbers 16, God killed 14,700 people because they were coming against Moses and Aaron. God told Moses to gather twelve rods from each tribe and said "And it shall be that the rod of the man whom I choose will blossom. Thus I will rid Myself of the complaints of the children of Israel, which they make against you" (Number 17:5). It was decided that God chose Aaron's rod. Then God spoke to Aaron and told him that he and his sons and the tribe of Levi "would bear the iniquity related to the sanctuary, and you and your sons with you shall bear the iniquity associated with your priesthood" (Numbers 18:1). God commissioned Aaron and his sons to the priesthood. Now what does this means to the ministry of the arts? After we have the written Word (*logos*) and the revelatory or revealed Word (*rhema*), we can operate in the power and authority of God (*dumas* and *exclusia*). We have been given the authority and power associated with the priesthood (or the ministry of the arts).

Once we know the written Word and what God is saying to us first and then to the people, we can operate in that authority and the power of God will meet us. No Word, No Power!

When we deal with choreography, you have to understand that everyone has a language or vocabulary. The people who are Hispanic speak Spanish and the inhabitants of China speak Chinese. Dancers have their own type of language. This is why I believe choreography is called core-ography because this is coming from the core of who you are or the core of who you believe God is. I STRONGLY believe God is a man of war and king, so it didn't so happen that my dance I am called for which is warfare. Now I learned my dance techniques because of being on the stage and in dance classes, but my belief system of who God is and the power behind the technique was developed in having an intimate relationship with God (studying, praying and even thru trials and tribulations). Use your testimony on what God has done for you thru your dance. If you know that God is faithful, show us that God is faithful. If you know that you have the victory or you have freedom, display that with your body, emotions and spirit. You are a tri-part being; you are a spirit, you have a soul and you live in a body. You are first a spirit; therefore, you must worship Him in Spirit and truth.

God is a Spirit (a spiritual Being) and those who worship Him must worship Him in spirit and in truth (reality) (John 4:24)

Everyone cannot see Spirit so communicate to your audience thru your body and soul (your emotions and feelings), which is the part everyone can see.

It is important that you are also physically, mentally and spiritually fit to do certain types of choreography; mentally fit would indicate that you are focused and physically fit means that you are able to properly execute the choreography. Practicing basic dance techniques and exercise would assist you in being physically fit. It is crucial that you take good care of your body because it is the only one you have and you use your whole body as an instrument to and for the Lord.

We have to deal with song selection. All songs are not made to be danced. Also, Top 40 Gospel songs are not always the best choice. The song must <u>first</u> minister and touch you as a messenger so you may be able to feel the message in your spirit, soul and body. It is in the heart where you must minister from. You are being vulnerable and naked before God in worship but now you are displaying it before the people of God.

When you are choreographing for a group, you have to take in the group; everyone's dance skills are not the same. Understand that you as a choreographer may have to modify the movements for your people. Also, group members, keep in mind that choreography is to stretch you as well. Sometimes, you have to go outside your comfort zone in order to minister to the audience.

For example, I remember assisting a particular dance ministry for a hip hop piece and one of the members stated "We are not used to this. We are worshippers."

Even though it was acknowledged, it was outside of their comfort zone, they still did it to the best of their abilities and anything that was EXTREMELY too much, then you would need to modify it.

As a team, everyone has their strengths and weaknesses. When you are coming up with choreography, make sure that you use everyone's strength and incorporate that within the piece.

Always know that when you are going before the people, you always have the Word of God hidden in your heart on what God is saying to His people because the Word of God is your source and this is your message as well as your own testimony. Don't short change the people and give them a good performance and no one don't receive the message that you are trying to convey. Always understand everyone is not going to understand or accept your message; if this should happen, just shake the dust off your feet. You did your job by conveying the message; if it is not received well, then that is not on you.

Chapter Six

Dancing with a Purpose

Now, let's discuss the different type of dances.

First, I want to establish this "genre" of dance. This whole book is based on liturgical arts. Liturgical is a root word for liturgy. Liturgy means public display of worship. So, liturgical dance is the public display of worship to God thru dance.

When we discuss the different types of dances, all of it is under the umbrella of liturgical dance. So when you say that you are just a praise dancer limits you to this particular type of dance. When you say that you are a liturgical dancer, it just signifies that you have dedicated your dance for God's glory, whether it is hip-hop, African, tap, jazz or any other technical types of dance.

The tongue has the power of life and death, and those who love it will eat its fruit. (*New International Version,* Proverbs 18:21)

When we wear shoes, we have the flap of the shoes which is called the tongue. So this scripture also refers to our feet; our feet are speaking life and death thru our dance. So in your dance, what are you speaking?

After consulting the people, Jehoshaphat appointed men to sing to the LORD and to praise him for the splendor of his holiness as they went out at the head of the army, saying: "Give thanks to the LORD, for his love endures forever." As they began to sing and praise, the LORD *set ambushes against the men of Ammon and Moab and Mount Seir who were invading Judah, and they were defeated* (*New International Version*, II Chronicles 20: 21-22)

Please understand that when you operate in the ministry, you are on the front line of battle. I <u>strongly</u> say this, especially with youth involved doing warfare dance, if they are spiritually unaware of what they are doing and not strong enough to engage, you are leading sheep to the slaughter.

The various dances within liturgical dance are praise, worship, warfare, celebratory, ceremonial, intercession/travail, prophetic and encouragement.

What is important with liturgical dance is you must know who you are directing your dance to. Anytime you are ministering thru dance, you are overall communicating to God and to the people of God and sometimes to the enemy.

Praise Dance

"praise him with timbrel and dancing" (*New International Version*, Psalm 150:4).

Praise is a command from the Lord; He stated "*Let everything that has breath praise the* LORD" (*New International Version*, Psalm 150:6). Anyone can praise God with a shout, clap, and jump. This type of dance displays on WHAT God has done.

Worship Dance

"God is spirit, and his worshipers must worship in the Spirit and in truth" (*New International Version*, John 4:24).

Worship REQUIRES intimacy. This type of dance requires the dancer to have an intimate relationship with God. This type of dance displays WHO God is and what is your response to that revelation. When you display worship, you are displaying to the people your own personal relationship with God. Make sure when you do a ministry piece, you believe in the words that the song is saying and you have that communication line with the Father.

Warfare Dance

Warfare is uplifting God while denouncing the Kingdom of Darkness. The purpose of this dance is to pull down strongholds and *to proclaim freedom for the captives and release from darkness for the prisoners* (Isaiah 61:1). This physical display is reminding the enemy that he is under our feet. Movements involve sharp movements such as punching, kicking, stomping and leaping.

The LORD is a man of war: the LORD is his name. (*KingJamesVersion,*Exodus15:3)

In warfare, we are representing God as a man of war; therefore anytime we engage in this dance, we should have the resemblance of our Father!

And I will give thee the treasures of darkness, and hidden riches of secret places, that thou mayest know that I, the LORD, which call thee by thy name, am the God of Israel. (King James Version, Isaiah 45:3)

This is a specific nugget that I have to give: God will <u>never</u> send you into warfare without obtaining something! The purpose of going into war is not for you to just get into a fight on a consist basis and you have never gained anything. In the Book of Joshua, they were in war to obtain land; David went to war to purse after the enemy for taking the women, children and plunder (see I Samuel 30). In American history, after the Civil War, it was the end of slavery and restoration took place, which to the nation we know it as the Reconstruction period. With the American Revolution, America was fighting to be free from the British so we could become the United States. So when God is causing you to go to war, what are you gaining from it and who is being liberated by it?

Celebratory/Ceremonial Dance

Celebratory dance is done to celebrate a victory that has been won and *to proclaim the year of the LORD's favor and the day of vengeance of our God (New International Version, Isaiah 61:2).* An example of a celebratory dance would be David winning his battle over Goliath and Miriam dancing after the Pharaoh's chariots and horsemen were drowned.

Ceremonial dance is used during the times of special occasions such as weddings, funerals, baby showers and ordinations.

Intercession/Travail Dance

Intercession/Travail is used during the times of intercession. This requires the knowledge of intercession. Intercession is going in between the gap or praying for someone else; in this type of dance, you are actually praying thru your dance. This is the aspect of having a prayer line is essential for the dancer because you are interceding for someone else. The greatest form of intercession was when Jesus was on the Cross, taking upon the sins of the world. As an intercessory dancer, you must be able to sacrifice yourself for someone who may not know how or what to do; sometimes you may have to intercede for someone who does know God. Another side of intercessory dance connects with encouragement dance: being able to fulfill a need.

Encouragement Dance

Encouragement dance is the type of dance that you encourage your brother or sister. This would follow under *to comfort all who mourn, and provide for those who grieve in Zion* and *to bind up the brokenhearted* (*New International Version*, Isaiah 61: 1, 2).

Prophetic Dance

Prophetic dance requires the dancer to know the voice of God and the ability to flow with the Spirit of God. This type of dance may also be known as spontaneous. The dancer must have an understanding of the prophetic itself. You can have pieces that are choreographed; what makes pieces prophetic is not only when you are stepping outside of choreography and do whatever the Spirit of God leads you but also when you arrive at a place and the piece that you do is a specific word for the audience at that specific time. God may even change the piece that you were going to do and have you do something completely different.

Since the different types of dances have been explained, I want to add a disclaimer where God specifically have dancers set apart for specific type of dancers. For example, I am called for warfare and operate in the prophetic and intercession strongly; it is confirmed by God and it is displayed in the pieces that I do. Even though, I know that I am called in this area, I don't limit myself because God is not a God of limitations so I don't limit myself to this but I am open to operate in any direction God guides me.

Chapter Seven

Our Arsenal

As we are operating in the ministry of dance, we must understand that we have to be dressed properly.

Let's first establish the foundation of garments:

Exodus 28 is where we reference to the purpose and excellence of garments. We would pull things from this chapter as well as other scriptures for you to have an understanding of garments.

Have Aaron your brother brought to you from among the Israelites, along with his sons Nadab and Abihu, Eleazar and Ithamar, so they may serve me as priests. (New International Version, Exodus 28:1)

We start at verse one when God told Moses to gather Aaron and his sons to serve God in the office of the priest. We understand that in this book that you have to be selected by God in order for you to operate in the ministry of the arts.

#1:Garments are sacred.

….sacred garments [appointed official dress set apart for special holy specials] for honor and beauty (The Amplified Bible, Exodus 28:2, emphasis added)

Your garments are set apart specifically for ministering thru dance. You cannot treat your garments any kind of way because you are going specifically for the King and you have a hold in the middle of the top. These garments are not for you to walk around the street and just for you to look cute.

#2: Garments are holy.

When the priests enter the Holy Place, they shall not go out of it into the outer court unless they lay aside there the garments in which they minister, for these are holy, separate, and set apart. They shall put on other garments before they approach that which is for the people (The Amplified Bible, Ezek. 42:14)

And when they go out into the outer court to the people, they shall put off the garments in which they ministered and lay them in the holy chambers, and they shall put on other garments, lest by contact of their garments with the people they should consecrate (separate and set apart for holy use) such persons [unintentionally and unfittingly] (The Amplified Bible, Ezek. 42:19).

You have to recognize that your garments are holy. This means that your garments are meant to be kept up.

#3: Garments represent your office.

Your pastor or minister wears preaching robes that represents their office; your garments represent your priestly office. You don't allow other people to borrow your garment and think that it is ok because it is as if you are allowing someone else to wear your underwear. It is personal.

Tell all the skilled workers to whom I have given wisdom in such matters that they are to make garments for Aaron, for his consecration, so he may serve me as priest. (*New International Version*, Exodus 28:3)

God informed Moses to call for the **skilled** workers. This is where the anointed seamstress comes in. The ministry of the arts needs the assistance of the seamstress; he or she will be the one that God chose to make garments for the ministry. Their heart is for the ministry and their desire for the ministry of the arts is to display God's glory and splendor. The garment is just an extension of your ministry piece. Make sure that you have an anointed seamstress that has the heart of the ministry; if you do not, pray that God will send you one.

And I have filled him with the Spirit of God, in wisdom and ability, in understanding and intelligence, and in knowledge, and in all kinds of craftsmanship. (*The Amplified Bible*, Exodus 31:3)

It is important in connected this scripture with Exodus 28 is that God wanted someone that was filled with the Spirit of God as well as wisdom and the ability to make in this scripture case the items of the Tabernacle. We should desire to have an anointed seamstress who has the Spirit of God as well as the wisdom and the ability to sew and have an understanding and intelligence of how to get the garment done. Along with the knowledge of the ministry, they would be able to utilize the craftsmanship that God has given them. This would also be a requirement for those who make our props. When God requires the best, it is just for Him to present His glory and splendor on the Earth.

These are the garments they are to make: a breastpiece, an ephod, a robe, a woven tunic, a turban and a sash. They are to make these sacred garments for your brother Aaron and his sons, so they may serve me as priests (New International Version, Exodus 31:4)

There are seven separate pieces that God had the skilled workers make:

- Breastpiece (or also known as the Breastplate)
- Ephod
- Robe
- Tunic
- Turban
- Sash
- Undergarments (will be mentioned later)

God specifically says on why each piece was created as the chapter progresses. I will just pull out of the scripture on the specific reason why God had a particular piece created.

Ephod

"Make the ephod of gold, and of blue, purple and scarlet yarn, and of finely twisted linen—the work of skilled hands. [7] *It is to have two shoulder pieces attached to two of its corners, so it can be fastened.* [8] *Its skillfully woven waistband is to be like it—of one piece with the ephod and made with gold, and with blue, purple and scarlet yarn, and with finely twisted linen.*

⁹ "Take two onyx stones and engrave on them the names of the sons of Israel ¹⁰ in the order of their birth—six names on one stone and the remaining six on the other. ¹¹ Engrave the names of the sons of Israel on the two stones the way a gem cutter engraves a seal. Then mount the stones in gold filigree settings ¹² and fasten them on the shoulder pieces of the ephod as memorial stones for the sons of Israel. Aaron is to bear the names on his shoulders as a memorial before the Lord. ¹³ Make gold filigree settings ¹⁴ and two braided chains of pure gold, like a rope, and attach the chains to the settings.

If we look at today's usage of the ephod, we would consider this as an overlay. Now, with this particular piece, God had the workers take two onyx stones and engrave the names of the sons of Israel in the order of their birth and he would put six on one stone and the remaining six on the other. God also instructed that the onyx stones were to be placed on the shoulders of the priest as a memorial to the Lord. When we also look at this, we can say that he would carry the burdens of the people.

Carry each other's burdens, and in this way you will fulfill the law of Christ. (New International Version, Galatians 6:2)

Also this is a sign of intercession because the priest would have to go before God on behalf of the people. We in the New Testament still have to go before God behalf of others because that is our assignment in the ministry of the arts and as well as believers.

Breastpiece (Breastplate)

"Fashion a breastpiece for making decisions—the work of skilled hands. Make it like the ephod: of gold, and of blue, purple and scarlet yarn, and of finely twisted linen. [16] It is to be square—a span[ ] long and a span wide—and folded double. [17] Then mount four rows of precious stones on it. The first row shall be carnelian, chrysolite and beryl; [18] the second row shall be turquoise, lapis lazuli and emerald; [19] the third row shall be jacinth, agate and amethyst; [20] the fourth row shall be topaz, onyx and jasper.[ ] Mount them in gold filigree settings. [21] There are to be twelve stones, one for each of the names of the sons of Israel, each engraved like a seal with the name of one of the twelve tribes.

[22] "For the breastpiece make braided chains of pure gold, like a rope. [23] Make two gold rings for it and fasten them to two corners of the breastpiece. [24] Fasten the two gold chains to the rings at the corners of the breastpiece, [25] and the other ends of the chains to the two settings, attaching them to the shoulder pieces of the ephod at the front. [26] Make two gold rings and attach them to the other two corners of the breastpiece on the inside edge next to the ephod. [27] Make two more gold rings and attach them to the bottom of the shoulder pieces on the front of the ephod, close to the seam just above the waistband of the ephod. [28] The rings of the breastpiece are to be tied to the rings of the ephod with blue cord, connecting it to the waistband, so that the breastpiece will not swing out from the ephod.

[29] "Whenever Aaron enters the Holy Place, he will bear the names of the sons of Israel over his heart on the breastpiece of decision as a continuing memorial before the Lord. [30] Also put the Urim and the Thummim in the breastpiece, so they may be over Aaron's heart whenever he enters the presence of the Lord. Thus Aaron will always bear the means of making decisions for the Israelites over his heart

before the Lord.

The breastpiece was used to bear the name of the sons of Israel over Aaron's heart as a continuing memorial before the Lord along with the ephod. The Urim and Thummin was in the breastpiece so any decision that God was make would be displayed over Aaron's heart. In the New Testament, we see the breastplate again when we refer to the whole armor of God in Ephesians 6.

..... *with the breastplate of righteousness in place...* (*New International Version,* Ephesians 6:14).

Also another significance of the breastplate is for us to protect our heart.

Robe

"Make the robe of the ephod entirely of blue cloth, [32] with an opening for the head in its center. There shall be a woven edge like a collar[1] around this opening, so that it will not tear. [33] Make pomegranates of blue, purple and scarlet yarn around the hem of the robe, with gold bells between them. [34] The gold bells and the pomegranates are to alternate around the hem of the robe.[35] Aaron must wear it when he ministers. The sound of the bells will be heard when he enters the Holy Place before the Lord and when he comes out, so that he will not die.
  (*New International Version,* Exodus 32:31-35)

The robe was required when he ministered. We see most mime ministers use robes as well as those in preaching ministry. We already have that understanding if you have a pastor or minister that constantly preaches in robes. When the robe is worn, that also represents that particular office. The bells were placed so that he could be heard while he was in the presence of the Lord as well as when he came out. "Holy to the Lord" was also the subscription that was on the robe as well.

Woven Turban

"Make a plate of pure gold and engrave on it as on a seal: holy to the Lord. Fasten a blue cord to it to attach it to the turban; it is to be on the front of the turban. It will be on Aaron's forehead, and he will bear the guilt involved in the sacred gifts the Israelites consecrate, whatever their gifts may be. It will be on Aaron's forehead continually so that they will be acceptable to the Lord.
(New International Version, Exodus 32: 36-38)

The tunic was made so that he may be able to beat the guilt of the offerings of the people. We in the New Testament would have to refer this into covering and guarding our minds. We would need to have to be mindful of the thoughts that go thru our head and continuously renew our mind.

Therefore, I urge you, brothers and sisters, in view of God's mercy, to offer your bodies as a living sacrifice, holy and pleasing to God—this is your true and proper worship. Do not conform to the pattern of this world, but be **_transformed by the renewing of your mind._** *Then you will be able to test and approve what God's will is—his good, pleasing and perfect will. (New International Version, Romans 12:1-2)*

Tunic and Sash

"Weave the tunic of fine linen and make the turban of fine linen. The sash is to be the work of an embroiderer. Make tunics, sashes and caps for Aaron's sons to give them dignity and honor. After you put these clothes on your brother Aaron and his sons, anoint and ordain them. Consecrate them so they may serve me as priests. (New International Version, Exodus 32:39-41)

The tunic and sash were created so that was created to give the priest dignity and honor. God was placed dignity and honor on the priest; God desires to use vessels of honor.

If a man cleanses himself from the latter, he will be an instrument for noble purposes, made holy, useful to the Master and prepared to do any good work. (New International Version, II Timothy 2:21)

Undergarments

"Make linen undergarments as a covering for the body, reaching from the waist to the thigh.⁴³ Aaron and his sons must wear them whenever they enter the tent of meeting or approach the altar to minister in the Holy Place, so that they will not incur guilt and die." (New International Version, Exodus 32:42-43)

God wanted them to have undergarments so that they would be covered.

Anytime God wants us to go before Him, He does not want us to feel guilt for worshipping Him by any reason. His desire is that we are totally covered when we go before Him and especially to His people; we would not serve as a distraction but a blessing.

"This is to be a lasting ordinance for Aaron and his descendants."(New International Version, Exodus 32:44)

Because we serve in this priesthood, this will be a continuing legacy for those involved in the ministry.

Now, I want to cover the practical aspect; I am stating these things so that you are not a distraction instead of a blessing.

- Make sure that your garments are clean <u>and</u> dressed.
- If you don't wear dance shoes and you are barefoot, make sure that your toenails are handled properly as well as your feet are not ashy.
- Make sure that all body parts are on lock down.
- Make sure your hair is nice and neat.
- Good hygiene is a plus!!

Also, you have to understand that specific garments mean a specific thing for a specific piece.

Let use talk about color. Colors represent a specific thing when we minister thru dance. It is important we wear the proper colors to go with the proper song.

Black	Sin, darkness, evil, Death, Mourning, Humility, God's Intercession and power, Hiding place, Shadow of God's wings	Lam 4:8; Mal 3:14; Jer 8:21; Psa 17:8; Psa 18:11;23:4; Psa 97:2; Rev 6:5b
Red	Blood of Jesus, Atonement, War, Consuming Fire, Redemption, Love	Jos 2:18, 21; Heb 9:12-14; Rev 1:5; 6:4; 12:3
Purple	Royalty, Kingship, Kingdom Authority, Dominion, Sonship	Ex 25:4; 28:8; Esther 8:15; John 19:2
White	Purity, Holiness, Righteousness, Light, Innocence	Psa 51:7; Eccl 4:8; Rev 19:7-8, 14
Yellow	Glory of God revealed,	Isa 51:11; 61: 3;

	celebration, joy	Heb 1:9
Gold	God's glory and deity, manifestation of God	Ex 37:6; 40:34-35; Rev 1:13-14
Green	New life, New beginning, prosperity, eternal life, restoration, health, healing, sowing and reaping	Psa 52:8; 92:14; Psa 37:35
Orange	Praise, power, passion, warfare	1 Chr 23:13; Psa 113:3
Silver	Redemption, God's Word	Ex 30:13-16; Psa 12:6; 1 Chron 28:14
Blue	Heavenly, Prophetic, Holy Spirit, the Word of God, Wind of God	Ex 24:10; Num 15:38
Brown	Man, Earth, repentance and	Gen 1:10; Esther 4:3;

	humility	Daniel 9:3-5
Rainbow	God's promise and covenant	Gen 9:13-17
Yellow, Orange and Red	Fire of God	Acts 2:3
Pink	Heart of Flesh	Ezekiel 36:26

Now that you understand garments and color, we cannot forget about props. We don't used props because it looks cute but we use them for special purposes.

Let me first established this: why must we use instruments that God in the air? It is because our enemy is in the air. In which in time past you walked according to the course of this world, according to <u>the prince of the power of the air</u>, the spirit that now works in the children of disobedience" (Eph. 2:2, KJV) So it is important as dancers and instrumentalists that we use our arsenal to shift atmospheres because we have that ability.

Also please be aware that all props reflects God or His personality; so when we use all prop we should hold it up high as if it was God Himself.

And Moses built an altar, and called the name of it Jehovah-nissi: (King James

Version, Exodus 17: 15).

And Moses built an altar and called the name of it, The Lord is my Banner; (The Amplified Bible, Exodus 17:15).

Flags and banners are used for identification. Back in the Old Testament, they used the banners to identify which tribe you were from. In this day and age, we have flags that are used to identify what nation that we represent. We use banners and flags to declare in the atmosphere who God is and what God has done.

Sometimes, flags will have symbols on them actually has specific meaning on it. This is why it is important for everyone to have an understanding of symbols. For example, if we see a dove, we connect it to peace or the Holy Spirit based on Matthew 3:16. A harp or a lyre would be a symbol for intercession; one reference would be when David was playing the harp before Saul in I Samuel 16:23. Another example is I own "The Blood of Jesus" flag. This flag is the picture of Jesus' hand on the Cross and His blood is coming from his hand. This flag represents redemption and in warfare, this would also speak in the atmosphere saying "Satan, the Blood of Jesus is against you."

Streamers were used in times of warfare. What they used to do was when the air was strong they would use the streamers to see where they can shoot their arrows. When we use streamers, we would use it for praise, worship and warfare. In the Biblical aspect, streamer would represent flashes of lightning or streams of fire. The manifestation of this would be Acts 2:2 and Revelation19:6-7.

Tabrets (or glory hoops) are used to shift the atmosphere for the prophetic to occur as well as times of celebrations. The tabret is also considered as the "arrow of the Lord" (Stauss, 2005). Scripture references for this prop would be 1 Samuel 10:5-6, 1 Samuel 18:6 and II Kings 13:15-19.

Swords and staffs (rod or mat-teh') are symbols of authority. We would see the sword and staff in times of God's authority. Any example of God doing miracles with the staff (or rod/mat-teh') would be Moses in Exodus 4:2-20. God even says that He has a staff in Psalm 23:4. When we can look at the sword, it represents His Word. This can be referenced in Hebrews 4:12, Ephesians 6:17, and Revelation 19:11-16.

Billow Cloth is a long cloth that is handled by two people. The billow cloth represents the presence of God. We would see the billow cloth in times of worship or even prophetic declarations. This would also be a physical representation of the Holy Spirit overshadowing a person like the Holy Spirit or the power of God overshadowed Mary in Luke 1:35.

Crowns and specters represent the Kingship of God or Jesus. This would be displayed in the time of worship and to reverence to the presence of God.

Everything that we do in this ministry represents something. It is important that as a minister of dance that you know exactly what to use and when to use it.

Chapter Eight

Authority of a Dancer

*But God chose the foolish things of the world to shame the wise; God chose
the weak things of the world to shame the strong.(New International
Version, I Corinthians 1:27)*

Let's define the word *authority*:

"the power to determine, adjudicate, or otherwise settle
issues or disputes; jurisdiction; the right to <u>control</u>,
command, or determine. a power or right delegated or given;
<u>authorization</u> persons having the legal power to make
and enforce the law (Dictionary.com)

We see authority everywhere we turn. We see authority when the
police pull us over to give us a ticket; we see authority when we are in
a meeting and a person is speaking and no one else is speaking. This
chapter, I am going to focus on the authority of a dancer. I need to
first yell loudly: **YOU HAVE AUTHORITY AS A DANCER!!!**
Where did this revelation come from?

*So Herodias nursed a grudge against John and wanted to kill him. But she was
not able to, because Herod feared John and protected him, knowing him to be a*

*righteous and holy man. When Herod heard John, he was greatly puzzled; yet he liked to listen to him. Finally the opportune time came. On his birthday Herod gave a banquet for his high officials and military commanders and the leading men of Galilee. When the daughter of[1] Herodias came in and **danced**, she pleased Herod and his dinner guests. The king said to the girl, "Ask me for anything you want, and I'll give it to you." And he promised her with an oath, "Whatever you ask I will give you, up to half my kingdom." She went out and said to her mother, "What shall I ask for?" "The head of John the Baptist," she answered. At once the girl hurried in to the king with the request: "I want you to give me right now the head of John the Baptist on a platter." The king was greatly distressed, but because of his oaths and his dinner guests, he did not want to refuse her. So he immediately sent an executioner with orders to bring John's head. The man went, beheaded John in the prison, and brought back his head on a platter. He presented it to the girl, and she gave it to her mother* (New International Version, Mark 6:19-28, emphasis added)

Did you see it?!?!? Herodias' daughter **_DANCED_** and the king said that I will give you whatever you want!!! You have got to understand the authority that you have as a dancer!! You have got to hear me!! Exotic dancers understand this strongly!! They operate in the authority to have men and women give them money at their feet for their own purpose and have these men and woman chasing after them. We know God and we have the anointing on our side!! What is our problem?? It's because we don't know **OUR AUTHORITY**!! We don't know our influence!!

From the beginning, I have expressed to you about having the heart and pure motives for ministry. This is why; if you don't have the right motives for this ministry, you will abuse it and someone may actually get killed (or beheaded). Here is my question to you: What are you going to do with the power that God has given you as a dancer? What is going to be your purpose for your dance?

I pray that you understand this point before I go to the next one. In order for us to go into territories or do anything that is a part of our vision, we have got to know that we have authority to operate in ALL God said that we can do!

For I myself am a man under authority, with soldiers under me (New International Version, Matthew 8:9a)

This is the key for you to operate in authority; you must know how to submit under authority. This may be tough for a LOT of people because the authority that you are under, you don't even want to be there. It is important that you are under a pastor that is teaching you the Truth, which is the Word of God. Whatever you submit yourself under, you will manifest that in your dance. I personally say that because I was ministering thru dance at a particular event and a mother of the church told me after the event, she thanked God for my ministry piece that I presented because she received and thank God for the teaching that my pastor is giving me because I would not be able to dance or operate in that anointing if it wasn't for his teaching.

Understand this: It is important that you have the RIGHT teaching for what you are doing. We see that Herodias told her daughter to tell the king "Give me John's head." The authority had ill purposes. This is important for you to know this because you must submit to whatever your leadership says, even though God has anointed you and given you authority. If leadership is abusive, then God will handle them from mishandling their authority and the fruit of their leadership will be manifested.

The last thing that I need to mention about the authority of a dancer is know that we have authority over the world.

At the center of all this, Christ rules the church. The church, you see, is not peripheral to the world; the world is peripheral to the church. The church is Christ's body, in which he speaks and acts, by which he fills everything with his presence (*The Message Bible*, Ephesians 1:22-23).

The world is peripheral to the Church!

Here is the best example for this; I will refer to anatomy for this. We have the nervous system, which is composed of two parts: the central nervous system (CNS) which is the brain and spinal cord and the peripheral nervous system (PNS) which is composed of other nerves in our bodies. Now, the brain and the spinal cord control (or sends signals) to the peripheral nervous system; this means that the brain and the spinal cord is telling the peripheral nervous system what to do. So in this light, the Church is supposed to be telling the world what they are supposed to be doing!

The world is supposed to be submissive to the Church. We as the Church should be setting the example by operating in excellence and power but here is a news flash: the world thinks that your artistic gifting and purpose of serving God is a joke because we don't understand authority!!

We are copying competitive television shows such as *So You Think You Can Dance* and *America's Best Dance Crew* and has adopted this in the Church, not realizing that we are causing competition between brothers and sisters in Christ. The sad thing is the contestants of those shows actually display a type of camaraderie and don't do a lot of foolishness that we carry on and do.

Do this: slap yourself, hit your left arm, hit your right arm, hit your chest, and hit your knees. This would look crazy if someone was looking at you doing this, right? Now view the other person is God and you are the Body of believers. This is exactly how we look like to God! We are fighting ourselves!

God didn't give us authority for us to be a lord over ourselves; He gave us authority for the purpose of His Kingdom being advanced by fulfilling the vision that He placed in us! We are not accomplishing anything but us fighting against ourselves. My pastor stated something awesome over the pulpit one Sunday: "Whenever people are quarrelling, they don't have a vision." When we are continuously fighting with each other, we lost our vision.

Once you understand what true authority is within yourself and you operate in that authority by submitting to someone else, then you would be able to make an effective change in the world.

Chapter Nine

Theatre/Drama

What is theatre? Theatre really is a place that displays or projects a world of imagination, making it tangible. The functions of theatre are highly influential: religious purpose, therapeutic use, entertainment and education. Theatre is a part of the artistic world that has many adversities but still has survived. Theatre has incorporated many things such as music and dance into productions and has expanded greatly into different varieties of genres and outlets. This chapter is exploring the journey of the theatre from the past to the present, foresight of the future and how to apply this area into ministry.

First, theatre started with religion. All theatre practitioners should know that our forerunners, the Greeks and Romans, did theatre as a form of worship to Dionysus or Bacchus the god of wine, revelry and fertility. There comes a belief that there is a type of spirit that is connected to different plays. The play may evoke entertainment or a life lesson to cause an audience member to be changed. Peter Senkbeil, a professor of theatre at Concordia University and a board member of Christians in Theatre Arts believes that there is no such thing as Christian theatre—but he also sees all arts as religious regardless of it is from a religious viewpoint. "I think there's some kind of spiritual dimension in all theatre" (Collins-Hughes 2006). Today, theatre has some type of religious roots connected to it somewhere.

Theatre used for religious purpose has truly made an impact on theatre today. In the Middle Ages, The Church had productions called "morality plays" to teach morality and right character but at some point the church cut the theatre away because the plays were becoming more secular. Now since we are in the new millennium, the church has decided there has to be another creative way of reaching the people, therefore deciding to go back to the theatre. It is a great concern to me that theatre may be taken out of the church again because of unexpected results for the church.

A revolution that needs to happen concerning theatre in the Church is that it needs to become more focused on the teaching and reaching out aspects instead of always preaching at the audience. Many playwrights have accomplished this and have gotten the results that they desire. People need to stop being very narrow minded about how to portray reality and the message together. Some people need to know how to effectively minister through drama for the groups they are trying to reach out to instead of doing an illustrated sermon for the church. For example, having a preacher or pastor do an extremely long monologue forces the people to think that they are in church. I heard comments from theatre students say that when they see this take place, they feel like they are in the wrong place and at that point everything is over their head or they completely shut down and don't have a good response to the monologue itself. This is what is going on. I agree with some people that not everybody needs a degree in order to operate in the gift of drama ministry but I believe that in order for you to understand the fullness of this gift, you must have some type of constructive criticism on how to make your talent or gift better. The purpose for conferences and workshops is to further your understanding about your talent and gift and how you can operate in it more effectively. A child with a great gift has to grow up in his gift in order to understand it and operate in the fullness of it.

Another side of theatre that is not viewed is the therapeutic drama which is known as "drama therapy." There are people that use theatre as a type of therapy to release emotions and to become a better person. This type of drama gives someone a deep view of themselves and causes them to have a transformation in their personal, emotional life. These people need whole-hearted and honest theatre, not some type of cheap performance.

Relationships are the foundation of a successful play or theatre production company which, to me, describes immediate theatre. Peter Brook's The Empty Space mentions Immediate Theatre. This is the relationships between the actors and the audience and also relationships between the actor and the director. The relationship between an actor and an audience member is a personal relationship based on honesty and truth that an actor plays his or her character. This is where you would hear statements from audience members to the actor that the role that he or she played spoke to them in some kind of way and the character that the actor played was a reflection of the audience member; you may actually hear the audience member say, "When I saw you, I saw myself." This type of relationship not only requires the truth and honesty of the actor but the attention and participation of the audience member as well. This is the most essential relationship in all of theatre because it is the working of the relationship between the actor and the audience member that causes the theatre to continue to stay alive. Other relationships are between an actor and a director, between an actor and a stage manager, and an actor and technical support such as dressers and running crew. These are very loose relationships. I have seen abuse between these relationships because some actors figure that because they are the "star" of the show, they can treat anyone any kind of way with yelling, screaming and fussing. This is where my personal statement needs to be said, "When it comes to the artistic world of theatre, there is no need for divas with dysfunctional attitudes." There has been too much focus on the actor and very little attention to those who are operating behind the scenes.

Theatre is a team effort. The director has a vision for the production he or she is doing and the actor submits to the vision that the director has. The stage manager backs up the director by running the show when the show opens and the actor has to listen to the stage manager to look presentable. The technical support such as running crew and dressers are to help the show run smoothly so the actor does not have to worry about costume or scenery concerns and can stay focused on being in character and establishing the relationship between the audience. There are no such things as "stars," but artists who strive to accomplish a vision for the theatre.

Now since that I have given the foundation for the theatre, I want to give you a blueprint on how you can make your drama pieces or your theatre ministry effective.

It first starts with the writer, or playwright, writing the script. My strongest advice to you, the writer, is that IT HAS TO BE REALISTIC!! If you make your piece in a fantasy world, then make sure you stay in that universe. For example, if you want your piece to be about fairies, please don't have Abraham Lincoln, the Vampire Slayer, somewhere in the midst. We are just visiting a world that we don't know anything about it, so you must introduce each character and element to us so we can understand what is going on. Writer, make sure that you have a purpose of why you are writing this. What is the message you want to convey in this piece? How are you going to convey the message that you want to bring?

From the writer, it goes into the producer's hand. Let's acknowledge the producer; the producer secures the rights of the play (if the playwright isn't someone you know, then you would have to ask the playwright permission to produce and direct the play). The producer hires the director, designers, actors and crew. The producer also secures finances to assist the play. The producer, in some cases, is the director as well. If the producer hands the play to a specific director, then the producer would hand the script to the director. The director reads it and hopefully the director loves the writer's script. This is the place where the director, tries to make the script realistic, where the vision becomes real.

The director makes sure that his production team consisting reads the script and after the production team has read it, the production team, consisting of all designers and stage manager gets a production concept of what they individually see from their artistic area. For example, the costume designer gets an idea what costumes he or she wants for the characters and the scenery designer then has an idea what the stage would look like. Once the production concept is developed, then the director meets with his production team and has a production meeting, where the director tells his team what the vision is for this piece. From that, the production team builds from this as well as informs the director what their ideas are. This production team is composed of: the technical director, lightning designer, sound designer, scenery designer, prop master and costume designer. The technical director oversees the technical team; the costume designer is responsible for the constructing and gathering costumes for the play, the prop master is responsible for gathering the props for the play. The scenic designer is responsible for construction and making the stage come to life. The sound designer gathers all the sounds for the piece, which includes music and sound effects. If it is a musical, then you need to include the musical director. Of course, the music director is responsible for the singing aspect as well as the musicians. What is very important, director, is that your team is skillful in what they do.

After the production meetings have a general direction on what they want to do, the director now has auditions for actors. Actors, please understand that the purpose of earning a role is for you to display the characters in the script. If you get a role that is outside of your natural character, then you would have to do research on how to make your character realistic. You, as the actor, must tell us the background story of the character, which is your responsibility. You must know your character's habits and behavior to display that on stage.

Now that everyone has been selected, we have to go into the rehearsal process. This is a time where the director and actors have time to work on making the script come to life. When the time comes close to the opening night of the show, technical rehearsals need to be done. Technical rehearsals are when all the technical elements, costume, light, sound and scenery come together. The first technical rehearsal is a paper tech, a rehearsal where the light, set, sound and costume designers come together with the stage manager and create cues for the show. A cue is when something specific happens on stage that very moment, such as the set changes or character wears another costume. After the paper tech has been done, a dry tech, a run-through without the actors, takes place. Once the dry tech is completed, a wet tech, which is the first time the actors and all the technical elements, except the costumes, will come together for the first time. Here the actors interact with the lights, set and sound. After the wet tech is done, dress rehearsals are performed. Dress rehearsals are run-throughs where the actors wear the costumes and makeup; this leads up to the final dress, the rehearsal right before the show. Director, I just want to make you aware that the wet tech and dress rehearsals may prove to be difficult but don't be frustrated because this is the first time everything is coming together and everything will be fine. Now it is the opening of the show, you break all your legs and arms to give it your best. After the show is completed and over, you must do strike, which is cleaning up, tearing down the set, and putting the costumes up.

In this chapter, I also wanted to briefly mention human video. Human video is how theatre and dance become one. This is where the drama and dance ministry come together and they minister off a song. The drama ministry acts out certain aspects of the song and the dance ministry dances off the song. Many times, if there is not a separate ministry of dance and drama, then the dance or drama does it all. The best way to describe human video is watching a music video in a live performance. All the elements of theatre are still needed for this time of ministry since acting is required in this act form.

This may be a lot of work involved, but there is complete satisfaction in this area. The hard work wasn't for anything, especially if you touch audience members' lives.

Chapter Ten

Real Men Do Worship

(Men of Worship and Warfare)

God has established men to have dominion on Earth and to be a role model for the people of God. According to Jewish customs, it was the man's role to lead worship as well as public religious rituals. What has happened is that the enemy has made a lie come into the man's mind that worship is feminine and, of course, it seems like the truth because the majority of the time, women are always displayed in this ministry. When it comes into disarming the lie, the man must see a demonstration of men worshipping thru the arts. Understand that all men will not worship the same way. I am a man from the theatre and God has anointed me for this area. I am confident in this; therefore, I move in it. What I want to show in this chapter is that God used various men in the Bible to establish worship while operating in authority, displaying boldness, and doing physical demonstrations of worship.

In order for a man to bring liberation to another, he must have experienced the presence of God personally. Moses experienced the presence of God at the Burning Bush.

"The Angel of the Lord appeared to him in a flame of fire out of the midst of a bush; and he looked, and behold, the bush burned with fire, yet was not

consumed. And Moses said, I will now turn aside and see this great sight, why the bush is not burned. And when the Lord saw that he turned aside to see, God called him out of the midst of the bush and said, Moses, Moses! And he said, Here am I. God said, Do not come near; put your shoes off your feet, for the place on which you stand is holy ground" (Exodus 3:2-5).

Moses took off his sandals and covered his face to show his reverential fear to the Lord.

In the personal experience, God will give you the assignment He has for you and how to conduct it. This caused God to commission Moses to be a deliverer to the nation of Israel and to confront Pharaoh. Exodus 3:10 says, *"Come now therefore, and I will send you to Pharaoh, that you may bring forth My people, the Israelites, out of Egypt."* According to Egyptian culture, Pharaoh was believed to be the son of Ra, the sun god. When God told Moses to confront Pharaoh, it was because he was confronting a form of false worship as well as holding on to the children of Israel.

In the midst of his worship, God gave Moses instructions on how to conduct or how to handle his assignment. Exodus 4:1-5 says, *"And Moses answered, But behold, they will not believe me or listen to and obey my voice; for they will say, The Lord has not appeared to you. And the Lord said to him, What is that in your hand? And he said, A rod. And He said, Cast it on the ground. And he did so and it became a serpent [the symbol of royal and divine power worn on the crown of the Pharaohs]; and Moses fled from before it. And the Lord said to Moses, Put forth your hand and take it by the tail. And he stretched out his hand and caught it, and it became a rod in his hand, [This you shall do, said the Lord] that the elders may believe that the Lord, the God of their fathers, of Abraham, of Issac, and of Jacob, has indeed appeared to you."*

After the plague of the death of the firstborn and Israel was released, Pharaoh was chasing the children of Israel. Moses stretched his rod and his hand over the sea and God caused it to be divided for the children of Israel to walk on dry land. Moses did the same thing and it caused the sea to come down on the Egyptians with their chariots and horsemen devoured by the water in Exodus 14:26.

Another sign began to happen: when Moses lifted up his hands, the Israelites were winning but when his hands were being lowered, the Amalekites were winning. Exodus 17:11 denotes, *"When Moses held up his hand, Israel prevailed; and when he lowered his hand, Amalek prevailed."* This is an indication that in the midst of worship, we say we surrender so God can fight our battles. Our focus on the Lord during worship causes God to vindicate His children in battle. These particular signs were happening because Moses lifted up his hands. Psalm 141:2 says, *"Let my prayer be set forth as incense before You, the lifting up of my hands as the evening sacrifice."* Always know that any time God gives you your assignment, He has already given you what you need to accomplish the assignment.

Being a man of warfare and worship qualifies him to be exalted to minister to another. David was known as a man after God's own heart.

"But now your kingdom shall not continue; the Lord has sought out [David] a man after His own heart, and the Lord has commanded him to be prince and ruler over His people, because you have not kept what the Lord commanded you" (I Samuel 13:1).

Because David was a man after God's own heart, God said that he was going to become king. God's desire is that he has men in leadership to lead His people into worship. When God sent an evil spirit to Saul, it was advised to him that he had a cunning harp player to dispel the evil spirit that was tormenting Saul. This demonstration of worship or music from a man of warfare and worship shows that it causes tormenting spirits to cease.

"And when the evil spirit from God was upon Saul, David too a lyre and played it; so Saul was refreshed and became well, and the evil spirit left him" (I Samuel 16:23).

A man of worship and warfare operates in authority. In his many demonstrations of the authority of God on his life, Moses used a staff (rod). According to Strauss (2005), the Hebrew word for rod is mat-teh' . The mat-teh' means the "divine government rod of authority " or "the rod of God." "In Exodus 7: 17-20, God used the symbolic rod in the hands of Aaron, a human ambassador, to render judgment in the form of turning all the water in Egypt to blood. It became a rod of judgment over the Egyptians' foreign gods and punishment to the people who worshipped them. As Aaron performed the enactment on the earth as directed of the Lord, with the rod in his hands, he was shadowing what the Lord was doing with the rod (mat-teh') that was in His hand in the heavenly realm."

Another sign of authority is the shofar. "In the story of Gideon and his men, found in Judges chapters 6 and 7, it is not beyond the realm of possibility that when the men blew on their ram's horns, symbolic of the voice of the Lord, and broke the pitchers covering the lamps, symbolizing the Father of lights coming into their midst, there was so much noise, (vibrations targeted at the Midianites) in the spiritual realm that it terrorized the enemy into a chaos and panic. They declared with a shout the prophetic word that the Lord had given Gideon in chapter 7 verse 9: The sword of the Lord (the divine-heavenly), and of Gideon (humanity-earthly), were in unity, to defeat their enemies" (Strauss, 2005). "Horns are a symbol of governmental authority throughout the scripture" (Strauss, 2005). Using physical props such as the rod and shofar displays the physical manifestation of the spiritual authority of a man of worship and worship.

A man of worship and warfare seeks the Lord. "The word 'seek' means to search, try to discover, request, look for or aim at. It actually implies that we desire to seek something or someone, and we do not seeking it until we connect properly with that person or revelation. How do we *seek* God's face? We are to use every dimension of prayer and worship that we know" (Pierce and Dickson, 49). David was a good example of this; when he arrived home from Ziklag, he found out that everything had been taken captive. After he encouraged himself in the Lord, First Samuel 30:7-8 says, "*David said to Abiathar the priest, Ahimelech's son, I pray you, bring me the ephod. And Abiathar brought him the ephod. And David inquired of the Lord saying, Shall I pursue this troop? Shall I overtake them? The Lord answered him, Pursue, for you shall surely overtake them and without fail recover all.*"

King Josiah was also a man that sought God.

"*And the king commanded Hilkiah the priest, Ahikam son of Shaphan, Achbor son of Micaiah, Shaphan the scribe, and Asaiah servant of the king, Go, inquire of the Lord for me and for the people and for all Judah concerning the words of this book that has been found. For great is the wrath of the Lord that is kindled against us because our fathers have not listened and obeyed the words of this book, to do according to all that is written concerning us*" (II Kings 22:11-12).

Because of this, the Word of the Lord to King Josiah that because he had a tender heart, rent his clothes and cried to the Lord, he would go to his grave in peace and he would not see the evil that the Lord would bring into the land.

Solomon was another man that sought the Lord. God told him in Second Chronicles 7:14, "*If My people, who are called by My name, shall humble themselves, pray, seek, crave, and require of necessity My face and turn from their wicked ways, then will I hear from heaven, forgive their sin, and heal their land.*" "The act of seeking is part of worship" (Pierce and Dickson, 2002). Seeking the Lord is also a sincere sign of worshipping the Lord.

A man of worship and warfare has to pull down or destroy something in order to establish true worship. According to Pierce and Dickson (2002), "The Lord understood that the Jewish people were not adequately established in worship. Therefore, He did not want them to go out by the way of the land of the Philistines "lest perhaps the people change their minds when they see war, and return to Egypt" (Exod. 13:17). God knew He would have to establish a worship pattern in them before they were confronted with other enemies; otherwise, they would retreat into an old pattern and their former lifestyle."

While Moses was on the Mount Sinai, he received the Ten Commandments, which were the Israelite laws on how to conduct themselves before the Lord. The first commandments that the Lord said: "You shall have no other gods before *or* besides Me. You shall not make yourself any graven image [to worship it] or any likeness of anything that is in heavens above, or that is in the earth beneath, or that is in the water under the earth; You shall not bow down yourself to them or serve them; for I the Lord your God am a jealous God, visiting the iniquity of the fathers upon the children to the third and fourth generation of those who hate Me, But showing mercy *and* steadfast love to a thousand generations of those who love Me and keep My commandments" (Exodus 20:3-6).

Once the Lord has established this law, the people wanted Aaron to make gods to go before them because they didn't know what happened to Moses. Aaron took the gold ear rings from the wives, sons and daughters and made a molten calf. In verses 19 and 20,

"And as soon as he came near to the camp he saw the calf and the dancing. And Moses' anger blazed hot and he cast the tables out of his hands and broke them at the foot of the mountain. And he took the calf they had made and burned it in the fire, and ground it to powder and scattered it on the water and made the Israelites drink it." After this, Moses said, "Whoever is on the Lord's side, let him come to me. And all the Levites [the priestly tribe] gathered together to him (v.26). Moses then instructed the Levites to kill all of those that wasn't on the Lord's side. From that day, about 3000 men fell.

Another great example of this is Elijah on Mount Carmel. In First Kings 18:19 and 21, Elijah said to Ahab, "therefore send and gather to me all Israel and Mount Carmel, and the 450 prophets of Baal and the 400 prophets of [the goddess] Asherah, who eat at [Queen] Jezebel's table." "Elijah came near to all the people and said, 'How long will you halt *and* limp between two opinions? If the Lord is God, follow Him! But if Baal, then follow him.' And the people did not answer him a word." With a man of worship and warfare, there are not gray areas; either you are going to worship the Lord God fully or not at all.

When Elijah confronted the false prophets, in verses 37-40, he says, *"'Hear me, O Lord, hear me, that this people may know that You, the Lord, are God, and have turned their hearts back [to You]. Then the fire of the Lord fell and consumed the burnt sacrifice and the wood and the stones and the dust, and also licked up the water that was in the trench. When all the people saw it, they fell on their face and they said, The Lord, He is God! The Lord, He is God! And Elijah said, Seize the prophets of Baal; let not one escape. They seized them, and Elijah brought them down to the brook Kishon, [as God's law required] slew them there."* With this example, God had Elijah eliminate the false governmental system of worship in order for the worship of the True and Living God to be reinstated.

The next man of worship and warfare that connects with this is Gideon. When God told Gideon that he was a "mighty man of [fearless] courage" and that He would use Gideon to save Israel from the hand of Midian, Gideon tested and proved the Word of the Lord. After Gideon received the Word of the Lord, Judges 6:25-26 says, *"That night the Lord said to Gideon, Take your father's bull, the second bull seven years old, and pull down the altar of Baal that your father has and cut down the Asherah [symbol of the goddess Asherah] that is besides it; And build an altar to the Lord your God on top of this stronghold with stones laid in proper order. Then take the second bull and offer a burnt sacrifice with the wood of the Asherah which you shall cut down."* This was bold for Gideon to do this because the men of the city wanted to kill Gideon because he pulled down the altar of Baal and cut down the Asherah. After pulling down the Baal altar and sacrificing the Asherah, Gideon built an altar to the Lord and called it "The Lord is Peace." According to Pierce and Dickson (2002), "From this place of worship, God revealed Himself not only to Gideon, but also to Israel in a way He has never revealed Himself before. He is declared as Yahweh Shalom, the Lord Is Peace. This character of God would bring about Israel's wholeness, security, well-being, prosperity and realignment. Worship released this empowerment."

Josiah was an eight-year-old king who reigned in Jerusalem for thirty-one years and did what was right in the sight of the Lord; once he found out about the Law of Moses when he was eighteen, he did all he could to establish true worship back into the land. Second Chronicles 23: 4-15 and 19-25 says that King Josiah *"commanded Hilkiah the high priest and the priests of the second rank and the keepers of the threshold to bring out of the temple of the Lord all the vessels made for Baal, for [the goddess] Asherah, and for all the hosts of the heavens; and he burned them outside Jerusalem in the fields of the Kidron, and carried their ashes to Bethel [where Israel's idolatry began]*.

He put away the idolatrous priests and idolatrous practices, such as male cult prostitutes houses, child sacrificing and worshipping idol statutes.

Jesus even did a demonstration of correcting and demonstrating what is true worship. Matthew 21:12-13 says, *"And Jesus went into the temple (whole temple enclosure) and drove out all who bought and sold in the sacred place, and He turned over the four-footed tables of the money chargers and the chairs of those who sold doves. He said to them, The Scripture says, My house shall be called a house of prayer; but you have made it a den of robbers."* As you can see, men of worship and warfare have to be bold when it comes to worshipping the True and Living God. Pulling down false worship and establishing true worship is part of the duty of a man of worship and warfare.

A man of worship and warfare physically displays worship and it causes God to respond. After Gideon worshipped and returned to the camp of Israel and informed the camp that the Lord had given the Midianites into their hands.

"When I blow the trumpet, I and all who are with me, then you blow the trumpets also on every side of all the camp and shout, 'For the Lord and for Gideon!' So Gideon and the 100 men who were with him came to the outskirts of the camp at the beginning of the middle watch, when the guards had just been changed, and they blew the trumpets and smashed the pitchers that were in their hands. And the three companies blew the trumpets and shattered the pitchers, holding the torches in their left hands, and in their right hands the trumpets to blow [leaving no chance to use swords], they cried, the sword for the Lord and Gideon! They stood every man in his place round about the camp, and all the [Midianite] army ran—they cried out and fled. When [Gideon's men] blew the 300 trumpets, the Lord set every [Midianite's] sword against his comrade and against all the army, and the army fled as far as Beth-shittah toward Zererah, as far as the border of Abel-meholah by Tabbath" (Judges 6:18-22).

God said in Psalms 47:1 "O *clap your hands, all you people! Shout to God with the voice of triumph and songs of joy!"* and Psalm 98:6 says "*with trumpets and the sound of the horn make a joyful noise before the King, the Lord!"*

Another man that operated in this is Joshua. He received his commanding orders from the Lord from worship.

"And He said, No [neither], but as Prince of the Lord's host have I now come. And Joshua fell on his face to the earth and worshiped, and said to Him, What says my Lord to His servant? And the Prince of the Lord's host said to Joshua,

Loose your shoes from off your feet, for the place where you stand is holy. And Joshua did so." (Joshua 5:14-15)

In the midst of Joshua's worship, God commanded Joshua in Joshua 6:3-5, *"You shall march around the enclosure, all the men of war going around the city once. This you shall do for six days. And seven priests shall bear before the ark seven trumpets of rams' horns; and on the seventh day you shall march around the enclosure seven times, and the priests shall blow the trumpets. When they make a long blast with the ram's horn and you hear the sound of the trumpet, all the people shall shout with a great shout; and the wall of the enclosure shall fall down in its place and the people shall go up [over it], every man straight before him."* When the people of God shouted and the trumpets blew, Jericho's wall fell down and the Israelites went into the city and took it. Gideon and Joshua won their battles because of their shouts.

Shadrach, Meshach and Abednego were men of worship and warfare who didn't use a shout or dance in this midst of their battle but what they did have boldness to stand against false worship and stand for the True and Living God.

"Shadrach, Meshach, and Abednego answered the king, O Nebuchadnezzar, it is not necessary for us to answer you on this point. If our God Whom we serve is able to deliver us from the burning fiery furnace, He will deliver us out of your hand, O king. But if not, let it be known to you, O king, that we will not serve your gods or worship the golden image which you have set up!" (Daniel 3:16-18).

In the midst of their devotion to God and stand against the false worship, God protected them while they were in the furnace and was exalted.

"He answered, Behold, I see four men loose, walking in the midst of the fire, and they are not hurt! And the form of the fourth is like a son of the gods!" (Daniel 3:25).

"Then Nebuchadnezzar said, Blessed be the God of Shadrach, Meshach, and Abednego, Who has sent His angel and delivered His servants who believed in, trusted in, and relied on Him! And they set aside the king's command and yielded their bodies rather serve or worship any god except their own God. Therefore I make a decree that any people, nation, and language that speaks anything amiss against God of Shadrach, Meshach, and Abednego shall be cut in pieces and their houses be made a dunghill, for there is no other God who can deliver in this way! Then the king promoted Shadrach, Meshach, and Abednego in the province of Babylon" (Daniel 3: 28-30).

Solomon also displayed physical action through prayer.

"When Solomon had finished praying, the fire came down from heaven and consumed the burnt offering and the sacrifices, and the glory of the Lord filled the house. The priest could not enter the house of the Lord, because of the glory of the Lord had filled the Lord's house. And when all the people of Israel saw how the fire came down and the glory of the Lord upon the house, they bowed with their faces upon the pavement and worshipped and praised the Lord, saying, For He is good, for His mercy and loving-kindness endure forever" (II Chronicles 7:1-3).

When a man (or men) of worship and warfare operates in his true authority as a worshipper, God will respond to him (or them) by protection and exaltation.

Jehoshaphat, another man of worship and warfare, used worship as his tactic for warfare.

"And Jehoshaphat bowed his head with his face on the ground, and all Judah and the inhabitants of Jerusalem fell down before the Lord, worshiping Him" (II Chronicles 20:18).

"When he had consulted with the people, he appointed singers to sing to the Lord and praise Him in their hold [priestly] garments as they went out before the army, saying, Give thanks to the Lord, for His mercy and loving-kindness endure forever! And when they began to sing and to praise, the Lord set ambushments against the men of Ammon, Moab, and Mount Seir who had come against Judah, and they were [self-] slaughtered; For [suspecting betrayal] the men of Ammon and Moab rose against those of Mount Seir, utterly destroying them. And when they had made an end of the men of Seir, they all helped to destroy one another (II Chronicles 20:21-23). Jehoshaphat established the principle that the praise team or the worshippers would go first when it is time to go to battle; this wise man has now given us the term where the worship and arts ministries are the front line soldiers in battle. With these physical acts, it caused God to respond in a mighty way.

God said that he would restore the Tabernacle of David. Acts 15:16-17 says "After this I will come back, and will rebuild the house of David, which has fallen; I will rebuild its [very] ruins, and I will set it up again, so that the rest of men may seek the Lord, and all the Gentiles upon whom My name has been invoked."

According to Pierce and Dickson (2002), "Whereas the Tabernacle of Moses was for the Israelites along, the Tabernacle of David included both Jew and Gentile.

(1) David's Tabernacle pointed us toward a new covenant filled with grace and faith.

(2) David's Tabernacle pointed us to a new Church order, where all believers could be kings and priests. David demonstrated this.

(3) David's Tabernacle, after the dedication, shifted from animal sacrifices to sacrifices of joy, thanksgiving and praise.

(4) David's Tabernacle became the habitation of the Ark of God's presence until the Temple was completed.

(5) David's Tabernacle had the Ark of the Covenant and foretold of someone who would come and sit upon the Throne forever.

(6) David's Tabernacle didn't have a veil, so there was access. This represented mediation and intercession.

(7) David's Tabernacle had singers, musical instruments and songs of praises within the confines of the tent. A new order and continual sound of worship arose.

(8) David's Tabernacle opened the door for the coming of all nations. Whether you were circumcised or uncircumcised, you had access to this tabernacle.

Pierce and Dickson (2002) continue to say "When God says He is restoring the Tabernacle of David, He is not bringing us to an Old Testament order. He is just making sure that everything is shifted from the Law of Moses' tabernacle to the prophetic life-giving power that we find in David's Tabernacle."

"God's intent has been to raise up the level of worship that David established in the Tabernacle to use as a weapon of warfare in these last days to possess all the nations of the earth" (Pierce and Dickson, 2002).

According to Dimitrov (2008), "After that he appointed priests, musicians, singers, etc, and commanded them to offer God sacrifices, but not animal sacrifices. The Bible says he even made instruments for the musicians, and he commanded them to offer the sacrifices of singing, praise and worship, praying, and playing on the instruments before God. See? He didn't offer animal sacrifices inn his Tabernacle (except on the dedication day), but he appointed courses of musicians (thousands of them), so they can Praise and Worship the Lord God of Israel 24 hours a day." David's Tabernacle as a model for worship is going to be restored.

Men of worship and warfare have often been men to make significant marks throughout history. These biblical examples of worshipping men are just an encouragement to other men to be conscious and focused on worshipping God. While men are worshipping God, it is a direct implementation that God is fighting the battle for us as well. Seeing worshipping men in public encourages the culture to worship God as well because it brings God's divine order to where He wanted the men to lead worship.

Chapter Eleven

Structure of the Arts

This is a VERY important chapter! I wanted to indicate that certain key things that must be indicated when it comes to the arts.

#1: Know those that labor with you.

And we beseech you, brethren, to know them which labour among you, and are over you in the Lord, and admonish you;(KingJamesVersion, I Thessalonians 5:12)

It is important that if you are a part of a ministry, you need to know your people. You need to know who they are and what their personalities are. I am not telling you that you have to be every one's best friend but in order for anyone to work together as an unit. You must know the people around you and you must know their purpose.

Leaders, it is imperative that you know your people. As a leader, you are responsible for them. This does not give you permission to rule with an iron fist and become a dictator. It is important that you continue to operate in love and gentleness. Members, regardless of past mistakes of your leader, you still must respect your leader and don't be so familiar with your leader that you completely disrespect the responsibility that they have over you. Understand that anything that happens on the behalf of the ministry, it falls on the leadership. Leadership is responsible for everything in the ministry and if leadership is constantly disrespected, it will become frustrating. It is important that all needs to understand the vision and purpose of the ministry as well as the gift and purpose of an individual.

#2: Stay in your lane!

He waited seven days, the time set by Samuel; but Samuel did not come to Gilgal, and Saul's men began to scatter. So he said, "Bring me the burnt offering and the fellowship offerings." And Saul offered up the burnt offering. ¹⁰ Just as he finished making the offering, Samuel arrived, and Saul went out to greet him. "What have you done?" asked Samuel. Saul replied, "When I saw that the men were scattering, and that you did not come at the set time, and that the Philistines were assembling at Mikmash, ¹² I thought, 'Now the Philistines will come down against me at Gilgal, and I have not sought the LORD's favor.' So I felt compelled to offer the burnt offering." "You have done a foolish thing," Samuel said. "You have not kept the command the LORD your God gave you; if you had, he would have established your kingdom over Israel for all time. But now your kingdom will not endure; the LORD has sought out a man after his own heart and appointed him ruler of his people, because you have not kept the LORD's command." (New International Version, I Samuel 13:8-13)

This is a ministry where everyone has their role to play. Each individual must know their role in the ministry and they must respect each other's role in the ministry. Everyone respects the role of their boss on their job; if not, the consequence of that is that you will be fired. We can look at Saul and saw that this is something that Saul highly disrespected and he was rejected as King! God is a God of order and He demands for that to take place even in the ministry.

#3: Understand the culture of the ministry

This is an area where competition tries to set in. Understand that everyone's ministry is NOT the same! Sadly, what happens is that because one church's culture means that if the dance ministry is only supposed to do special ministry pieces, then so be it. Other church's culture is that dancers are to dance during praise and worship and do special ministry pieces during services as well. Whatever the culture of the church is, submission must be a key factor when it comes into ministry.

What is the most important factor in everything is that we must always be in order whenever we operate in ministry.

#4: Restoration is important!

Let us not become conceited, provoking and envying each other. Brothers and sisters, if someone is caught in a sin, you who live by the Spirit should restore that person gently. But watch yourselves, or you also may be tempted. Carry each other's burdens, and in this way you will fulfill the law of Christ. (New International Version, Galatians 5:26- Galatians 6:1-2)

Please note that it is important that you reflect love and gentleness towards one another. Every form of team needs to be work together; it should be deeper because we are in the same family and we are worshipping the same God. We should be able to be there for one another and not abuse each other. We should not have to boast in ourselves but always be able to support each other and don't operate in judgment and condemnation.

#5: Appointment is always good!

It is always good for you to solicit and solidify someone to handle something in particular for the ministry. This takes away the stress of rushing and having to do things at the last minute. This also represents operating in the spirit of excellence. For example, if there is someone anointed for sewing, then there is your anointed seamstress in the midst of you. The whole purpose of you being able to use the people in the midst of you is so you would not have to stress about how something is going to get done. As well, that particular person is using the ability and gifting that God gave them to enhance the ministry. It is important that the ministry knows everyone in leadership position. If there is no one in the midst of you, then it is not wrong for you to get outside help.

#6: Getting outside help isn't wrong!

It is important that networking is not ungodly! It is important that you know your brothers and sisters in God as well as what are their gifts. This is a HUGE work that needs to be done and we cannot do it all by ourselves. One particular ministry cannot do it all! We as a collective whole need one another to be unified and be able to edify each other as well as engaging into fulfill the commission that God has given us. God is so much bigger than just the four walls of one church; He is a God of many cultures and He wants His children to be able to work together without any hindrances and distractions.

#7: Always operate in covenant.

Covenant is defined as a "formal and binding agreement entered into by two or more persons or parties; a compact" (Webster 2000). Covenant is an intimate relationship where one party is fulfilling the basic needs of every human being to the adjacent party; those needs are: acceptance (know that a person is loved and needed), identity (knowing that a person is specific and unique), security (knowing that a person is well-protected and trusted) and purpose (knowing a person is in the other person's life). Covenant is not like a contract; a contract is conditional but a covenant is unconditional and it requires blood shed (cleanliness). Jesus already shed his blood for us so we should have covenant with Him as well as our brothers and sisters in Christ (Huskins 2003).

#8: Be like Hannah!

Hannah could not conceive a child and after her prayer to the Lord and Eli told her that her request will be granted. She became pregnant with Samuel the prophet of Israel. After Samuel became weaned, Hannah dedicated Samuel back to the Lord. We should remember that God gave us this ministry and He can do what He wants.

These are just some tidbits that could assist you with the structure of the ministry.

Chapter Twelve

The Spirit of Excellence

These are the offerings you are to receive from them: gold, silver and bronze; [4]
blue, purple and scarlet yarn and fine linen; goat hair; [5] ram skins dyed red
and hides of sea cows; acacia wood; [6] olive oil for the light; spices for the
anointing oil and for the fragrant incense; [7] and onyx stones and other gems to
be mounted on the ephod and breastpiece. [8] "Then have them make a sanctuary
for me, and I will dwell among them. [9] Make this tabernacle and all its
furnishings exactly like the pattern I will show you. (New International Version,
Exodus 25:3-9)

From Exodus Chapter 25-31, God was instructing Moses about the
building of the Tabernacle. At this point in Israel 's history, God has
already delivered them out of Egypt . This is the most profound
thing I want to point out: God had the children of Israel build the
tabernacle **_WHILE_** they were in the Wilderness. He had them create
things from *"gold, silver, bronze, blue, purple and scarlet yarn and fine linen"*
and etc. (verse 3-7). In Exodus 31:3, He said that he called Bezalel
and Aholiab and had filled them with the Spirit of God, in wisdom
and ability. What am I saying, "In the midst of any type of situation,
especially in lack, **WE STILL HAVE TO OPERATE IN A
SPIRIT OF EXCELLENCE!**"

We as the Body of Christ procrastinate on some things. This is not
good! Diligence needs to be defined in this chapter. Dictionary.com

states that diligence means "constant and earnest effort to accomplish what is undertaken; persistent exertion of body or mind." We have to be constantly focused on our vision in order to reach our destination. God Himself doesn't do things half way. When we look at the creation in Genesis 1 and especially Genesis 2 when he created man and woman, He did it in excellence. The definition of excellence is "*The quality of being excellent; state of possessing good qualities in an eminent degree; exalted merit; superiority in virtue.*" (Dictonary.com). We serve an excellent God and He does things in excellence; He does this because I believe He wants His children to operate in that same level of excellence.

In a conversation, one of my state coordinators states: "*Everything we label as the enemy attacking us is not an attack moreso than it is a lack of our preparation. You know what I am saying and operating in a spirit of excellence and expectation, going ahead and do things that you know has to get done so everything can take place and be fruitful.*"

There is a word of wisdom to leaders whether it is arts ministry or arts organizations, take heed of the advice Jethro gave Moses (see Exodus 18:14-27). Choose some people who are able and will help you in your vision (or task). When you have huge tasks, you can't do everything by yourself. I learned my lesson; I had to ask one of my brothers who is skillful in graphic arts to create a logo that I need. I was going to attempt to draw and that is something I am not skillful in so the best thing was to hand it to someone who has the Spirit of God and the skillful wisdom that can handle it.

I also want to indicate God would not require you to get something that you don't have. We look at the materials and the prices of things that we need. God does not want you to go into debt or wants you to do something completely out of your budget in order for you to give Him glory. He knows where you are and what He does require from you is that you give him what you have and with that, He wants you to give it your best.

Please let us operate in a spirit of excellence because God always does things in a wilderness place.

Conclusion

I pray that everything that was said as a blessing for you and that you will be able to utilize these truths in your ministry.

Father I thank you and I glorify Your holy name that you used me a vessel to minister to this reader. I pray that now that they have the knowledge, they will be able to apply the knowledge to their ministry. I pray that the Spirit of God continues to be upon them and everything that is within this reader that you cause to flow out of them. I thank you for the anointing on his or her life and I praise you that as they will continue to live, move and have his or her being in You. May the uniqueness of this reader's ministry continue to flourish and the gates of Hell will not prevail. I thank you that their weaknesses are your strength; I thank you that the joy of the Lord is their strength. I thank you that their passion of you will continue to be ablaze and I pray that no weapon formed against this reader will prosper and every tongue that rises up against this reader, they shall condemn. Reader, you are covered by the Blood of Jesus and be encouraged to do the work of the Lord!

God Bless!

References

Anoint. (2009). In *Dictionary.com*. Retrieved 2009, from

http://dictionary.reference.com/browse/anoint?s=t

Asaff, S. (2006). Where Does Cinnamon Come From.

In *LovetoKnow Herbs*. Retrieved 2012, from

http://herbs.lovetoknow.com/Where_Does_Cinnam

on_Come_From

Authority. (2011). In *Dictionary.com*. Retrieved 2011, from

http://dictionary.reference.com/browse/authority?s=t

Brooks, P. (1996). *The Empty Space*. New York, NY:

Touchstone.

Calamus/Sweet Flag. (n.d.). In *The Epicentre*. Retrieved

2012, from

http://theepicentre.com/spice/calamus-sweet-flag/

Collins-Hughes, L. (2006, September). "Articles of

Faith." *American Theatre*, 30-33.

Dimitrov, Nikola (2008). *The Tabernacle of David*.
      Retrieved January 27, 2011, from
      http://www.articlealley.com/article_590370_51.html

Dockery, K., Godwin, J., & Godwin, P. (2000). *The Student*

Bible Dictionary (2000th ed.). Uhrichsville, OH:

Barbour Books.

Filippone, P. T. (2012). Cinnamon and Cassia Selection

and Storage. In *About.com*. Retrieved 2012, from

http://homecooking.about.com/od/foodstorage/a/cin

namonstorage.htm

Huskins, D. (2003). *The Purpose of a Covenant Heart*.

Shippensburg, PA: Destiny Image Publishers, Inc.

Motives. (2009). In *Dictionary.com*. Retrieved 2009, from

http://dictionary.reference.com/browse/motives?s=t

Nielsen, E. (1999). Different Mime Types. In *eHow.com*. Retrieved 2013, from http://www.ehow.com/list_6719160_different-

mime-types.html

Olive Oil. (2012). In *eNotes.com*. Retrieved 2012, from

http://www.enotes.com/olive-oil-reference/olive-oil

Pierce, C. D, & Dickson, John (2002). *The Worship*

Warrior. Ventura, CA: Regal Books.

Strauss, J. (2005). *Heavenly Impact: Symbolic Praise,*

Worship, and Intercession (3rd ed.) Quincy, MI:

Publisher Glorious Creations.

The American Educator Encyclopedia (1967). FLY. Lake

Bluff, IL: The United Educators Inc..

The New International Webster's Pocket Dictionary of the

English Language (2000 ed.).

Uttley, C. (1998). *How Poetry Works*. In *How Stuff Works*.

Retrieved,2013,from

http://entertainment.howstuffworks.com/arts/literature/poetry1.htm

Wallace, K. (1993). *History of Step Dance*. In *eHow.com*. Retrieved 2013, from http://www.ehow.com/about_5095238_history-step-dance.html

Zavada, J. (2012). What is Myrrah?. In *About.com*.

Retrieved 2012, from

http://christianity.about.com/od/glossary/a/Myrrh.htm

Biography

Julious Fletcher obtained his Bachelor of Fine Arts in Theatre Performance at Columbus State University in 2008. Under the mentorship of Apostle Veronica Smith, he completed the Free To Be Me Mentoring Program; a twelve month intensive program concerning persons who have a calling in the liturgical arts domestically and internationally. Julious is currently pursuing a Masters in Expressive Arts emphasis in Dance Therapy at Lesley University.

Julious is a member of a few dance organizations including Christian Dance Fellowship USA, which is a part of International Christian Dance Fellowship, International Dance Commission, and Christian in Theatre Arts. He has taught classes at several dance conferences i.e. hip hop, African dance, intercessory warfare dance, flags, drama and human video, to name a few.

Julious, also known as "Warrior Prince" because of his strong belief of God being Warrior and King, displays this belief through liturgical dance.

Through everything that Julious has been through, he will always believe that God is God and He still reigns on the throne.

www.ingramcontent.com/pod-product-compliance
Lightning Source LLC
Chambersburg PA
CBHW071232090426
42736CB00014B/3049